Do Not Judge

Jeremy Lopez

Do Not Judge

Published by Dr. Jeremy Lopez

Copyright © 2023

This book is licensed solely for your personal enjoyment only. This book may not be re-sold or given away to other people. If you would like to share this book with another person, please purchase an additional copy for each recipient. If you are reading this book and you did not purchase it or it was not purchased for your use only, please return to your favorite book retailer and purchase your own copy.

All rights reserved. This book is protected under the copyright laws of the United States of America. All information contained herein is the expressed intellectual property of Dr. Jeremy Lopez and Identity Network International. This book may not be copied or reprinted for commercial gain or profit. The use of short quotations or occasional page copying for personal or group study is permitted and encouraged.

ENDORSEMENTS

Jeremy does an excellent job of giving balanced instruction on how to meditate, and also explaining the benefits that come from having a regular meditation and mindfulness practice. I love how Jeremy is not afraid to learn from and quote those outside the Christian tradition. He is able to explain the ancient concepts simply from a Biblical perspective. – Kari Browning, Director, *The Beautiful Revolution*

You are put on this earth with incredible potential and a divine destiny. This powerful, practical man shows you how to tap into power you did not even know you had. – Brian Tracy – Author, *The Power of Self Confidence*

I found myself savoring the concepts of the Law of Attraction merging with the Law of Creativity until slowly the beautiful truths seeped deeper into my thirsty soul. I am called to be a Creator! My friend, Dr. Jeremy Lopez, has a way of reminding us of our eternal 'I-Am-ness' while putting the tools in our hands to unlock our endless creative potential with the Divine mind. As a musical composer, I am excited to explore, with greater understanding, the infinite realm of possibilities as I place fingers on my piano and whisper, 'Let there be!' – Dony McGuire, Grammy Award winning artist and musical composer

Jeremy dives deep into the power of consciousness and shows us that we can create a world where the champion within us can shine and how we can manifest our desires to live a life of fulfillment. A must read! – Greg S. Reid – *Forbes* and *Inc.* top rated Keynote Speaker

I have been privileged to know Jeremy Lopez for many years, as well as sharing the platform with him at a number of conferences. Through this time, I have found him as a man of integrity, commitment, wisdom, and one of the most networked people I have met. Jeremy is an entrepreneur and a leader of leaders. He has amazing insights into leadership competencies and values. He has a passion to ignite this latent potential within individuals and organizations and provide ongoing development and coaching to bring about competitive advantage and success. I would highly recommend him as a speaker, coach, mentor, and consultant. – Chris Gaborit – Learning Leader, Trainer

Dr. Jeremy Lopez's book Universal Laws: Are They Biblical? is a breath of fresh air and much needed to answer the questions that people have been asking about the correlation between Biblical and Universal Laws. I have known Jeremy Lopez for years, and as a Biblical scholar, he gives an in-depth explanation and understanding of the perfect blending and merging into the secrets and mysteries of these miraculous Laws and how Bible-based the Universal Laws truly are. As the show host for the past twelve years on The Law of Attraction Radio Network, this book answers questions that I have received from Christian and spiritual seekers around the globe about the relationship between the metaphysical and Biblical truths. After reading this book, readers will feel empowered and have strong faith that God has indeed given us these Bible-based Universal and Divine Laws to tap into so that we can live and create an abundant life. – Constance Arnold, M.A., Author, Speaker, Professional Counselor, Host of *The Think, Believe & Manifest Talk Show*

Table of Contents

Introduction	p.1
The Journey Within	p.21
The Seeds of Judgment	p.39
Connection Through Compassion	p.59
The Mirror Effect	p.77
The Art of Empathy	p.95
Freedom From Labels	p.113
Cultivating Mindfulness	p.131
Forgiveness and Letting Go	p.149
Embracing Diversity	p.169
A World Transformed	p.187
Conclusion	p.199

Introduction

"Judge not, that ye be not judged." The words are haunting, if you think about it. These words, found in the seventh chapter of the Gospel of Matthew, are a powerful reminder of the dangers of judgment – our judgment of others.

We think so often of the judgments of God on humanity, reminding ourselves that God is the supreme judge of all things. But have you ever stopped to consider just how often we being judgment upon our own selves because of our own judgments? Our judgments of others. Our judgments of life. Our judgments of literally anything and everything that we disapprove of.

The words in Matthews's Gospel serve as a stark warning of judgement. When we judge we bring judgment upon ourselves. This book, *Do Not Judge*, will share powerful revelation on what it means to live beyond the realm of judgment.

The verse "Judge not, that ye be not judged" is one of the most well-known and frequently quoted passages from the Bible. Found in the New Testament, it holds a profound message about human behavior, relationships, and the essence of Christianity. This chapter will explore the context, meaning, and implications of this verse, along with related passages, to gain a deeper understanding of the wisdom it imparts.

The verse in question can be found in the Gospel of Matthew, Chapter 7, verse 1 (Matthew 7:1), and it reads: "Judge not, that ye be not judged." This statement is part of the famous Sermon on the Mount, where Jesus delivers teachings to his disciples and the gathered crowd.

Before delving into the deeper meaning of this verse, it is crucial to examine its context within the Sermon on the Mount. In the preceding verses, Jesus addresses various topics such as hypocrisy, discernment, and the Golden Rule, highlighting the principles of righteousness and compassion. It is in this context that he imparts the caution against judgment.

The phrase "Judge not" is often misunderstood as a blanket statement against forming opinions or discerning right from wrong. However, a closer examination reveals that Jesus is primarily warning against a specific kind of judgment - one characterized by hypocrisy and a self-righteous attitude. In other words, Jesus advises his followers not to pass condemnatory judgments on others while ignoring their own faults.

This interpretation aligns with the subsequent verses in the same passage (Matthew 7:2-5), where Jesus illustrates the concept using a vivid analogy:

Verse 2: "For with what judgment ye judge, ye shall be judged: and with what measure ye mete, it shall be measured to you again." - This implies that the standard by which we judge others will be applied to us as well. If we are harsh and unforgiving in our judgment, we can expect the same treatment from God.

Verse 3-4: "And why beholdest thou the mote that is in thy brother's eye, but considerest not the beam that is in thine own eye? Or how wilt thou say to thy brother, Let me pull out the mote out of thine eye; and, behold, a beam is in thine own eye?" - Here, Jesus uses hyperbole to emphasize the absurdity of attempting to correct others' faults while ignoring more significant issues within ourselves.

Verse 5: "Thou hypocrite, first cast out the beam out of thine own eye, and then shalt thou see clearly to cast out the mote out of thy brother's eye." - In this verse, Jesus encourages self-examination and the acknowledgment of our imperfections before attempting to help others.

Jesus' message, therefore, calls for humility, self-awareness, and empathy in our interactions with others. It's not a prohibition on discernment but a reminder to approach others with compassion and understanding, recognizing our shared humanity.

To gain a comprehensive perspective on the theme of judgment, it is essential to examine other related verses in the Bible. Several passages echo the same sentiment and reinforce the teachings of Jesus:

Luke 6:37-38: "Judge not, and ye shall not be judged: condemn not, and ye shall not be condemned: forgive, and ye shall be forgiven."

This parallel verse from Luke's Gospel emphasizes the principle of reciprocity in judgment and forgiveness. By showing mercy and forgiveness, we create an environment in which the same kindness will be extended to us.

James 4:11-12: "Speak not evil one of another, brethren. He that speaketh evil of his brother, and judgeth his brother, speaketh evil of the law, and judgeth the law: but if thou judge the law, thou art not a doer of the law, but a judge. There is one lawgiver, who is able to save and to destroy: who art thou that judgest another?"

In this passage, James cautions against speaking ill of others and acting as judges, for ultimately, only God has the authority to judge. It echoes the idea of humility and refraining from passing unjust judgments.

Romans 14:13: "Let us not, therefore, judge one another anymore: but judge this rather, that no man put a stumblingblock or an occasion to fall in his brother's way."

Paul's letter to the Romans advises believers to avoid judgments that may harm their fellow brethren. Instead, the focus should be on promoting love and unity within the Christian community.

The verse "Judge not, that ye be not judged" encapsulates a profound spiritual truth that transcends religious boundaries. It reminds us of the importance of humility, self-reflection, and compassion in our relationships with others. By heeding this admonition, we can foster an environment of understanding and empathy, enriching our spiritual journey and positively impacting the lives of those around us. Through a careful examination of the context and related passages, we gain a deeper appreciation of the biblical wisdom behind this timeless verse, prompting us to embody its teachings in our daily lives.

As we reflect on the verse "Judge not, that ye be not judged," we must confront the reality of hidden judgments and biases that often exist within our own lives. Despite our best intentions, human nature tends to harbor preconceived notions and prejudices, affecting our perceptions and interactions with others. Here are some common ways we may unknowingly harbor judgments and biases:

Our upbringing and the culture we are immersed in play a significant role in shaping our beliefs and attitudes. Societal norms, stereotypes, and biases can seep into our subconscious, impacting how we perceive individuals from different backgrounds, races, or social classes.

This cognitive bias leads us to seek, interpret, and remember information that confirms our existing beliefs while disregarding evidence that challenges them. It can lead us to judge others based on incomplete or biased information, reinforcing preconceived notions.

Numerous studies in psychology have revealed the presence of implicit biases, which are automatic and unconscious attitudes that affect our judgments and behaviors. These biases can be related to race, gender, age, and other factors, leading us to treat certain individuals unfairly without even realizing it.

Sometimes, we project our own insecurities, fears, or shortcomings onto others. This projection can manifest in negative judgments about others, acting as a defense mechanism to avoid confronting our own issues.

Fear of the unknown or the unfamiliar can lead to judgments based on stereotypes rather than actual knowledge or experience. Ignorance about a person's background, culture, or beliefs can lead to misinterpretations and biased judgments.

Making constant comparisons between ourselves and others can create judgments about who is better or worse. Envy can breed negative attitudes towards those who possess qualities or possessions we desire.

Engaging in gossip or spreading rumors about others can lead to forming judgments based on secondhand information, often without considering the whole truth or the impact on the individual's reputation.

Recognizing and challenging our hidden judgments and biases is essential for personal growth and building stronger, more compassionate relationships with others. Here are some steps we can take to overcome these tendencies:

Regular self-reflection and mindfulness practices can help us become more aware of our thoughts, feelings, and biases. Being honest with ourselves about our judgments is the first step towards change.

Seek to understand and learn about different cultures, perspectives, and experiences. Education fosters empathy and helps break down barriers of ignorance.

Consciously challenge stereotypes and question assumptions we may hold about others. Engaging in open conversations and asking questions can help dispel misconceptions.

Put yourself in others' shoes and try to understand their experiences and feelings. Empathy builds bridges of understanding and promotes tolerance.

Avoid engaging in gossip or negative discussions about others. Focus on the positive aspects of individuals rather than dwelling on their shortcomings.

Embrace the richness of diversity and appreciate the unique contributions of each individual. Celebrate differences rather than judging them.

Recognize that every person deserves respect and dignity, regardless of their background or circumstances.

The verse "Judge not, that ye be not judged" is not a mere admonition but a profound call to examine our own hearts and behaviors. By acknowledging and addressing our hidden judgments and biases, we take steps towards personal growth and fostering a more inclusive, loving, and harmonious world. As we strive to live out the teachings of this verse, we can build bridges of understanding, extend compassion to others, and embody the true essence of Christianity - loving our neighbors as ourselves.

Living out the teachings of "Judge not, that ye be not judged" requires ongoing effort and a commitment to personal growth. As we continue on this journey of self-awareness and compassion, we can adopt specific practices to cultivate a non-judgmental mindset and break free from the shackles of biases.

Engage in mindful listening during conversations with others. Avoid interrupting or assuming you know what someone is going to say. Give them the space to express themselves fully, and listen with an open heart and mind.

Recognize that none of us is perfect, and we all have areas in our lives that require growth. Embracing humility helps us approach others with a sense of equality and understanding.

When you catch yourself forming judgments or entertaining biased thoughts, make a conscious effort to reframe them. Replace negative assumptions with more positive or neutral ones.

Whenever you find yourself reacting emotionally to someone's actions or words, pause and question the reasons behind your reaction. Are your feelings based on assumptions or genuine understanding?

Engage with people from different backgrounds and cultures. Interacting with individuals who have varied life experiences broadens our understanding and reduces biases.

Accept that imperfection is a part of the human condition. Rather than imposing unrealistic expectations on others, offer support and encouragement as they grow and learn.

The verse "Judge not, that ye be not judged" holds a profound significance in guiding us towards genuine relationships, empathy, and spiritual growth. It challenges us to look within ourselves, confront our hidden judgments and biases, and strive for a more compassionate and understanding demeanor.

As we commit ourselves to live according to this teaching, we contribute to a world that embraces diversity, inclusivity, and love. By adopting practices that cultivate non-judgmental attitudes, we pave the way for transformative change within ourselves and in the lives of those we interact with.

Let us remember that the journey towards shedding biases and judgments is ongoing. It requires self-compassion and patience as we unlearn ingrained habits and embrace a more enlightened way of thinking and being. With each step we take, we bring ourselves closer to the embodiment of Christ's teachings, fostering a world that reflects the love and acceptance He showed to all.

In our pursuit of embodying the teachings of "Judge not, that ye be not judged," we are called to create a culture of love, acceptance, and understanding. By embracing these principles, we can foster meaningful connections with others and promote harmony in our communities. As we continue on this transformative journey, let us explore further how we can integrate these values into our daily lives:

Just as we seek forgiveness and understanding from others when we stumble, we must extend grace to those around us. Recognize that everyone is on their own path of growth and may make mistakes along the way. Embrace an attitude of compassion and offer support when needed.

Instead of forming judgments and assumptions about others, engage in open and respectful dialogue. Seek to understand their perspectives, experiences, and emotions without imposing your own biases. Honest communication can bridge divides and build genuine connections.

Beyond individual actions, be aware of the existence of systemic biases and injustices in society. Advocate for equality and justice, and work towards dismantling oppressive structures that perpetuate discrimination.

Take a stand against discrimination in all its forms. Whether it's racism, sexism, homophobia, or any other form of prejudice, be an ally and advocate for those who face discrimination and marginalization.

To extend compassion to others, we must first be compassionate towards ourselves. Acknowledge that we, too, have flaws and areas for growth. Treat yourself with kindness and understanding, fostering a positive and empathetic mindset.

Embrace the beauty of diversity in all its forms - cultural, religious, ethnic, and more. Celebrate the unique qualities that each individual brings to the table and see them as valuable contributions to humanity's collective tapestry.

Support initiatives and programs that promote empathy education in schools, workplaces, and communities. By fostering empathy in the younger generations, we can create a more compassionate society for the future.

When conflicts arise, seek resolution through peaceful means. Avoid reacting impulsively and instead, approach the situation with empathy and a willingness to find common ground.

Cultivate an attitude of gratitude, recognizing the blessings in your life and the positive aspects of others. Gratitude helps shift our focus away from judgment and towards appreciation.

Engage in acts of service and kindness towards others without any expectation of reward. Small gestures of compassion can have a ripple effect, inspiring others to do the same.

The verse "Judge not, that ye be not judged" encapsulates a profound truth that transcends time and culture. It calls us to embrace humility, empathy, and love as we navigate the complexities of human relationships. By confronting our hidden judgments and biases, we create an environment where understanding and compassion thrive.

As we internalize these teachings and actively apply them in our lives, we become agents of positive change, not only for ourselves but for the world around us. Let us heed the call to let go of judgment and embrace acceptance, for in doing so, we foster a community where individuals are valued for their inherent worth and where love triumphs over prejudice.

In the spirit of this verse, may we strive to see the best in others, acknowledge our shared humanity, and embrace the diversity that enriches our lives. By living with an open heart and a non-judgmental mind, we can sow the seeds of harmony, understanding, and lasting transformation in the world.

The Journey Within

In this opening chapter, we will explore the concept of spirituality and its connection to the practice of not judging others. We will delve into the importance of self-awareness, understanding our biases, and cultivating a compassionate heart as the foundation for embracing non-judgment.

The human mind is a complex and intricate landscape, shaped by experiences, emotions, and beliefs. In this vast terrain of thoughts, we navigate not only through our inner world but also through the external world around us. One significant aspect of this mental journey is our judgment of others. How we perceive and evaluate others is not merely an objective observation but rather a reflection of the inner dynamics of our own psyche. This chapter delves into the depths of the mirror of judgment, exploring how the way we assess others mirrors our own inner world.

Judgment is an inherent human trait, evolved over millennia as a survival mechanism. Making judgments allowed our ancestors to discern between danger and safety, trust and suspicion. In the modern context, judgment still plays a vital role in our decision-making processes. However, when judgment extends beyond practical purposes, it can become a potent tool for self-reflection.

Perception is never neutral; it is filtered through the lens of our experiences, beliefs, and emotions. These filters shape how we interpret the actions and characteristics of others. When we judge someone positively, it often indicates that we see something in them that resonates with our own values or aspirations. On the contrary, negative judgments can reveal unresolved issues or insecurities within ourselves that we project onto others.

Carl Jung, the Swiss psychiatrist and psychoanalyst, introduced the concept of "projection." He theorized that we tend to attribute our own unconscious qualities, desires, and fears to others. In essence, what we reject or struggle to accept within ourselves, we often unconsciously project onto others. For example, if we harbor feelings of inadequacy, we might perceive others as arrogant or boastful to protect our self-esteem.

When we form judgments, we also identify with the characteristics we observe in others. This identification can be both positive and negative. Admiring someone's talent or compassion might indicate that we recognize similar qualities within ourselves. Conversely, feeling intense dislike for someone could indicate an internal struggle to come to terms with certain aspects of our own nature.

The "shadow self" is a Jungian concept that refers to the parts of ourselves that we suppress or deny, considering them undesirable or socially unacceptable. The shadow contains repressed emotions, desires, and traits that we disown but are still a part of us. When we judge others harshly for embodying these qualities, it can serve as a mirror to confront our own unresolved inner conflicts.

Society plays a significant role in shaping our judgments. Cultural norms, values, and expectations influence how we perceive and categorize others. In a culture that values competitiveness, we might criticize acts of kindness as weakness. Recognizing these influences can help us differentiate between our authentic judgments and those imposed upon us by external forces.

Just as negative judgments reveal our inner struggles, positive judgments and feelings of empathy also reflect our inner world. When we connect with others on a deep emotional level, it often signifies that we share similar emotions or experiences. Empathy acts as a mirror, allowing us to understand and relate to others by recognizing aspects of ourselves in them.

Becoming aware of the mirrors of judgment within ourselves requires deep self-reflection and mindfulness. By consciously examining our judgments, we can uncover the underlying beliefs and emotions driving them. This self-awareness offers an opportunity for growth and healing, allowing us to integrate the disowned parts of ourselves and promote greater self-acceptance.

The judgment of others is not a one-dimensional process; it is a multi-layered reflection of our inner world. Our perceptions are colored by the lenses through which we view the world, revealing our values, fears, and aspirations. By embracing the mirrors of judgment, we embark on a transformative journey of self-discovery and acceptance. Through empathy and compassion, we learn to recognize our shared humanity, fostering deeper connections with others and ourselves. As we continue to explore the intricacies of our inner landscape, we inch closer to living a more harmonious and authentic life.

As we embark on the journey of embracing the mirrors of judgment, we must recognize that self-reflection is not an easy task. It requires us to confront aspects of ourselves that we might have long avoided or denied. However, this process is essential for personal growth and healing. When we use judgment as a mirror, it becomes a powerful tool to delve into the depths of our psyche and unearth the treasures hidden within.

One of the primary keys to navigating the mirrors of judgment is self-compassion. Instead of criticizing ourselves for being judgmental, we should approach this exploration with gentleness and understanding. Self-compassion allows us to embrace our flaws and vulnerabilities with kindness, recognizing that they are part of our shared human experience. By showing compassion to ourselves, we create a safe space to confront our inner struggles and work towards transformation.

The journey of self-discovery through judgment leads us to confront the shadow self. These aspects of ourselves that we have repressed often hold immense power over our thoughts and behaviors. By shining a light on our shadow, we can begin to integrate these hidden parts of ourselves, leading to greater authenticity and self-awareness.

To fully understand the mirrors of judgment, we must explore the origins of our beliefs and biases. Our upbringing, cultural conditioning, and life experiences shape the way we perceive and assess others. Unraveling these roots allows us to differentiate between our genuine perceptions and those influenced by external factors.

Our childhood experiences play a pivotal role in shaping our judgments. The beliefs and attitudes we internalize from our caregivers, teachers, and peers become the foundation of our worldview. By revisiting these early imprints, we can identify the seeds of judgment that were sown in us and determine if they still serve us positively.

The media, social norms, and societal expectations significantly impact our judgments. Through constant exposure to certain ideologies and images, we absorb unconscious biases that color our perceptions of others. By becoming conscious of these external influences, we can challenge and reshape our judgments to align with our true selves.

Empathy serves as a transformative force in the journey of embracing the mirrors of judgment. By cultivating empathy, we not only deepen our understanding of others but also gain valuable insights into our own emotional landscape.

Practicing active listening and emotional intelligence allows us to attune ourselves to the feelings and experiences of others. As we genuinely connect with their emotions, we may recognize similar feelings within ourselves. This connection serves as a mirror that helps us identify shared experiences and emotions, promoting empathy and compassion.

Embracing the mirrors of judgment enables us to bridge the gap between ourselves and others. Instead of seeing people as separate entities, we begin to recognize the interconnectedness of all beings. By acknowledging our shared struggles and aspirations, we foster a sense of belonging and understanding.

As we delve deeper into the mirrors of judgment, we must seek ways to integrate our discoveries into our daily lives.

Cultivating mindfulness and self-awareness is essential in recognizing our judgments as they arise. By observing our thoughts and emotions without judgment, we gain clarity and insight into the root causes of our biases.

An open-hearted acceptance of diversity becomes a natural outcome of the self-discovery journey. As we acknowledge and embrace the unique qualities of others, we also learn to appreciate the richness of our own inner world.

The journey of embracing the mirrors of judgment is a profound expedition into the depths of our being. Through self-reflection, empathy, and compassion, we unravel the intricate layers of our inner world, bringing to light both our light and shadow selves. By recognizing that judgment is a reflection of our inner landscape, we open the door to personal growth, transformation, and greater connection with ourselves and others. This voyage is not without challenges, but the rewards are immense - a life lived with authenticity, empathy, and a deep sense of inner harmony.

In the Gospel of Matthew (Matthew 7:1-5), Jesus spoke about the concept of removing the mote from one's own eye before attempting to remove the speck from someone else's eye. This teaching highlights the importance of self-awareness and self-reflection before passing judgment on others. Let's explore this profound teaching and its relevance to the journey of embracing the mirrors of judgment.

In this teaching, Jesus used a powerful metaphor to illustrate the need for self-reflection before engaging in judgment. The "mote" represents a small speck or splinter, while the "beam" or "plank" symbolizes a much larger obstacle. By using this imagery, Jesus emphasized the disproportionality of scrutinizing others' faults while neglecting our own.

Acknowledging our own imperfections and vulnerabilities fosters humility. By humbling ourselves, we recognize that we are not above others but are fellow travelers on the journey of life. This humility allows us to approach judgment with greater compassion and understanding.

Jesus' teachings emphasized love, compassion, and understanding towards others. When we choose to remove the mote from our own eye, we adopt a Christ-like attitude of empathy and forgiveness. By seeing our own struggles and challenges, we become more attuned to the humanity and frailties of those around us.

The act of removing the mote from our eye is not just about self-improvement; it also has healing implications for our relationships. As we work on our own inner world, we create a ripple effect of positivity and transformation in our interactions with others. This healing presence can inspire others to engage in their own self-discovery journey.

The teaching of removing the mote from our own eye invites us to break free from the cycle of judgment and blame. When we focus on our internal growth, we shift our energy from criticizing others to bettering ourselves. This liberation from judgment allows us to experience greater inner peace and harmony.

Jesus' teachings often emphasized the unity of humanity and our interconnectedness. By removing the mote from our eye, we foster a sense of connection with others. We come to understand that our judgments not only impact us but also affect the collective consciousness of society.

In this chapter, we have explored the profound teaching of Jesus about removing the mote from our own eye before passing judgment on others. This teaching serves as a guiding light on our journey of embracing the mirrors of judgment. By delving into the depths of our inner world, cultivating empathy, and embodying Christ-like compassion, we transform the way we perceive and assess others.

As we continue to explore the mirrors of judgment within ourselves, let us remember the wisdom of Jesus' teaching and its relevance to our lives today. By removing the mote from our own eye, we embark on a path of self-awareness, humility, and healing. Through this transformative journey, we not only liberate ourselves from the burden of judgment but also contribute to a more compassionate and understanding world.

When we find ourselves quick to judge others, it is crucial to recognize the triggers that evoke such responses. These triggers often stem from unresolved issues within ourselves, such as past traumas, insecurities, or unhealed wounds. By acknowledging these triggers, we can begin the process of self-exploration and healing.

Mindfulness is a powerful practice that enables us to be fully present in the moment, observing our thoughts and emotions without judgment. By cultivating mindfulness, we become more aware of our automatic reactions to others and can interrupt the impulse to judge. Through this awareness, we create space for self-reflection and compassionate understanding.

As we confront the mirrors of judgment, it is essential to treat ourselves with compassion and kindness. Self-compassion involves being understanding and forgiving towards ourselves, just as we would offer compassion to a friend in need. By extending this kindness to ourselves, we dissolve the barriers that prevent us from accepting others without harsh judgment.

Nobody is perfect, and acknowledging our own imperfections allows us to relate to others with greater empathy. Embracing our flaws and mistakes as part of our human experience liberates us from unrealistic expectations and helps us view others through a lens of acceptance rather than judgment.

Truly listening to others is an act of empathy that fosters deep understanding. When we actively listen to their stories and experiences, we open ourselves to connecting with their emotions and perspectives. Through this empathetic engagement, we create an atmosphere of trust and compassion, paving the way for meaningful and transformative relationships.

Uncovering our own biases and assumptions is essential to overcoming judgment. We can question the validity of these beliefs and challenge them through exposure to diverse perspectives and experiences. By doing so, we broaden our understanding of the world and become more accepting of others' unique journeys.

The journey of overcoming judgment of others by looking within ourselves is a profound and transformative endeavor. By embracing the mirrors of judgment, we gain valuable insights into our inner world and recognize the interconnectedness of all human beings. Through self-reflection, mindfulness, and self-compassion, we liberate ourselves from the chains of judgment and foster a more compassionate and understanding mindset.

As we embody the wisdom of Jesus' teaching and integrate it into our lives, we contribute to a more harmonious and compassionate world. Let us embark on this inner quest with courage and open hearts, knowing that the journey of self-discovery and empathy will not only enrich our own lives but also positively impact the lives of those around us. May we continue to learn and grow as we walk the path of embracing the mirrors of judgment and fostering greater love, connection, and acceptance in our shared human experience.

The Seeds of Judgment

Understanding the origins of judgment is crucial to transcending it. In this chapter, we will explore how societal conditioning, upbringing, and personal experiences shape our tendency to judge others. By recognizing these factors, we can begin to dismantle the barriers that separate us from our fellow human beings.

As we embark on this profound journey of self-discovery, it is imperative to acknowledge that each one of us is an intricate tapestry woven from the threads of our environments and upbringings. In the grand tapestry of human existence, our individual stories unfold through a myriad of experiences, interactions, and influences that shape the very core of our being. We are products of our environments, molded by the subtle hands of our upbringing, and in understanding this, we can begin to grasp the essence of who we are and how we navigate the world.

The age-old debate of nature versus nurture has intrigued philosophers, scientists, and thinkers for centuries. While genetics lay the foundation for our inherent traits and capabilities, our environments and upbringings are the nurturing gardens that water the seeds of our potential. As we journey from infancy to adulthood, our experiences act as a sculptor, molding the contours of our personalities, beliefs, and values.

As we take our first breaths, we arrive as blank canvases, untouched by the strokes of life. The world around us is a cacophony of sensations, and in these early stages, we are highly impressionable sponges, absorbing everything we encounter. Our caregivers, often our parents, are our primary influencers during these formative years. The love and attention they provide lay the foundation for our sense of security and self-worth. The early bonds we form with them shape our future relationships, trust, and emotional development.

As we venture into childhood, the world becomes our playground, and our learning intensifies. School, friendships, and our surrounding communities become significant actors in our developmental play. The beliefs and values imparted by our families intertwine with cultural norms and societal expectations, creating the framework for our understanding of right and wrong. The experiences we have in these formative years influence our cognitive development, shaping our problem-solving skills, creativity, and emotional intelligence.

The tumultuous phase of adolescence marks a pivotal point in our lives. During this time, we grapple with questions of identity and belonging.

Our peer groups gain prominence, often introducing us to new ideas, trends, and beliefs that may challenge our earlier conditioning. The choices we make during this period are influenced by our desire to be accepted, to fit in, and to establish our independence from our families. It is a delicate dance between the teachings of our upbringing and the allure of exploration.

As we transition into adulthood, we begin to reflect on the unique tapestry that has been woven thus far. The experiences of our past, the lessons learned, and the scars endured all contribute to the amalgamation of our identities. The environment in which we were raised leaves an indelible mark on our worldviews, influencing our career choices, relationships, and overall life aspirations.

Acknowledging that we are products of our environments and upbringings does not imply that we are bound by them indefinitely. Humans possess an incredible capacity for growth, adaptation, and change. The awareness of our roots grants us the power to examine our beliefs critically, question our assumptions, and make conscious choices that align with our authentic selves.

While our environments and upbringings contribute to the essence of who we are, they can also foster limiting beliefs and patterns that hinder our personal growth. Unearthing these deeply ingrained ideas and behaviors can be challenging but rewarding. Therapy, self-reflection, and seeking support from others can aid us in breaking free from these confines and discovering our true potential.

In the grand tapestry of life, we are indeed the products of our environments and upbringings, shaped by the hands of nature and nurtured by the influences surrounding us. However, we are not mere passive recipients of these forces. We possess the capacity to learn, grow, and redefine ourselves throughout our journey. Embracing the complexity of our past, present, and future empowers us to paint new strokes upon the canvas of our lives and embrace the masterpiece that we are, ever-evolving and ever-adapting.

As we navigate the currents of life, we often find ourselves entangled in webs of judgment. From the earliest stages of our upbringing, society subtly shapes our perceptions, encouraging us to categorize people and situations into boxes of right or wrong, good or bad, acceptable or unacceptable. These judgments often go unnoticed, embedded deep within our subconscious minds, until the tapestry of our experiences begins to reveal their subtle threads. This chapter explores how the act of judgment, ingrained throughout our upbringing, can shape our beliefs, relationships, and self-perception, leading us to examine its unseen impact on our lives.

From the moment we are born, we are exposed to societal norms, cultural values, and family beliefs. These ingrained patterns serve as the framework for navigating the world, guiding our understanding of what is "normal" or "appropriate." Unfortunately, this process can also perpetuate harmful stereotypes and biases, influencing how we perceive others based on factors such as race, gender, religion, or socioeconomic background.

In childhood, we learn by observing those around us, especially our caregivers and authority figures. These individuals often become the benchmark for how we should interpret the actions and characteristics of others. For example, if we witness our parents expressing prejudice or making judgments, we are more likely to internalize these attitudes and replicate them in our own interactions.

As we mature into adolescence and adulthood, our inner landscapes become populated with self-doubt and insecurities. The judgments we have received from others, either explicitly or implicitly, can leave lasting imprints on our self-esteem. When we feel judged or criticized by our peers, colleagues, or society at large, we may start internalizing these perceptions, believing that we are somehow unworthy or flawed.

In an attempt to shield ourselves from judgment, we may engage in self-preservation strategies, adopting masks that we believe will make us more acceptable to others. These masks, however, distance us from our authentic selves, hindering genuine connections and genuine self-acceptance.

As we navigate the complexities of adulthood, we often become active participants in the cycle of judgment. Our ingrained biases and preconceptions unconsciously influence our perceptions of others, leading us to categorize people based on their appearances, behaviors, or beliefs. These judgments can shape our interactions, affect our relationships, and contribute to the perpetuation of discrimination and prejudice.

In addition to influencing our social interactions, judgment also impacts the decisions we make in life. Whether it's choosing a career path, pursuing a passion, or embracing our true identities, the fear of judgment from others can deter us from following our hearts and taking risks.

Becoming aware of the pervasive influence of judgment in our lives is the first step toward breaking free from its grasp. Self-reflection, mindfulness, and empathy play essential roles in this process. By examining our own prejudices and reflecting on the root causes of our judgments, we can begin to dismantle these preconceptions and replace them with openness and understanding.

Developing empathy allows us to see beyond the surface of others and connect with the shared humanity that unites us all. By putting ourselves in the shoes of others, we can better understand their experiences, struggles, and triumphs. As we cultivate compassion, we create a more inclusive and accepting world, one where judgment finds little ground to take root.

The unseen impacts of judgment run deep in the fabric of our lives, shaped by the influences of our upbringing and environment. From the seeds sown in childhood to the intricate patterns woven throughout our adult lives, judgment can affect our relationships, choices, and perceptions of self and others. Recognizing the far-reaching implications of judgment empowers us to challenge our preconceptions, cultivate empathy, and embrace our shared humanity. In doing so, we can begin to dismantle the walls that divide us, fostering a world where acceptance, understanding, and love reign supreme.

Embracing a journey of non-judgment is an arduous yet liberating path, one that requires introspection, humility, and a willingness to challenge deeply ingrained patterns. As we continue to explore the impacts of judgment on our lives, we delve into the transformative process of breaking free from the shackles of judgment. By cultivating self-awareness, practicing self-compassion, and fostering a culture of empathy, we can forge a new narrative that embraces the beauty of diversity, celebrates individuality, and nurtures authentic connections.

The journey of non-judgment begins with the courage to confront our biases and preconceptions head-on. Self-reflection acts as a mirror, enabling us to see the deeply-rooted beliefs that color our perceptions of the world. As we unpack our thoughts and emotions, we may discover uncomfortable truths about ourselves and our conditioning. It is crucial not to be judgmental towards these discoveries but rather view them as opportunities for growth and transformation.

Stereotypes thrive when we operate on automatic pilot, allowing them to dictate our interactions and decisions. As we embrace a journey of non-judgment, we must challenge these stereotypes consciously. Engaging with diverse perspectives and seeking to understand the stories of others help us humanize those we may have previously judged. By broadening our worldview, we open ourselves to the richness of human experience and dissolve the barriers that perpetuate misunderstanding.

Empathy acts as a bridge that connects us to the hearts of others, transcending differences and forging genuine connections. Developing empathy involves actively listening to others without judgment, acknowledging their emotions, and recognizing the validity of their experiences. It requires us to step out of our comfort zones and truly engage with the lives of those around us. As empathy becomes an integral part of our interactions, we lay the groundwork for meaningful relationships and a more compassionate society.

As we learn to let go of judgment towards others, it is equally important to extend the same compassion to ourselves. Embracing self-compassion involves accepting our imperfections, forgiving our mistakes, and treating ourselves with the same kindness we would offer a dear friend. When we release the burden of self-judgment, we liberate ourselves to embrace our authentic selves fully and lead more fulfilling lives.

Non-judgment thrives in an atmosphere of acceptance and inclusion. By celebrating the uniqueness of each individual, we create a space where diversity is cherished, and everyone can thrive authentically. Embracing diverse perspectives enriches our collective understanding and fuels innovation, creativity, and progress. It is through this appreciation of diversity that we can dismantle the barriers of judgment and build bridges of unity and harmony.

Breaking free from the chains of judgment is not solely an individual journey; it is a collective responsibility that extends to future generations. As parents, educators, and mentors, we play a vital role in shaping the minds and hearts of the next generation. By instilling values of empathy, compassion, and critical thinking, we empower young minds to question their assumptions and break free from the chains of inherited biases. By nurturing an environment that encourages curiosity, open dialogue, and understanding, we set the stage for a more tolerant and harmonious world.

The journey of non-judgment is not a linear path, but rather a continuous evolution of the self and society. As we unmask our biases, challenge stereotypes, and cultivate empathy and self-compassion, we weave a new narrative for ourselves and those around us. By embracing diversity, fostering acceptance, and nurturing future generations with empathy and understanding, we create a ripple effect that transcends boundaries and creates a more compassionate and non-judgmental world. The power to break free from the shackles of judgment lies within each of us, waiting to be harnessed for a brighter and more interconnected future.

As we continue our journey of non-judgment, we encounter a myriad of challenges and triumphs that test our resolve and commitment. The world we inhabit is diverse and complex, filled with contrasting ideologies, beliefs, and experiences. In this chapter, we explore the obstacles that stand in the way of non-judgment and celebrate the triumphs that arise when we consciously choose to embrace empathy, understanding, and acceptance.

One of the most significant challenges to non-judgment arises from the human tendency towards tribalism. We are drawn to those who share our beliefs, culture, and values, forming tight-knit groups that offer us a sense of belonging and security. However, this sense of unity can often lead to division and hostility towards those who are perceived as different.

Overcoming the us vs. them mentality requires us to recognize our shared humanity, find common ground, and bridge the gaps that separate us.

Cognitive biases are mental shortcuts that our brains employ to process information quickly. While they may have served evolutionary purposes, they can cloud our judgment and perpetuate stereotypes. Recognizing and challenging these biases requires a willingness to question our assumptions and engage in critical thinking. By cultivating a curious and open-minded approach, we can peel back the layers of preconceived notions and embrace a more nuanced understanding of the world.

As we navigate a world filled with diverse perspectives and complex challenges, it is easy to become overwhelmed. The constant influx of information, social media, and the fast-paced nature of modern life can lead to mental fatigue and emotional exhaustion. Practicing mindfulness and self-care become essential tools in maintaining our equanimity and focus. Mindfulness helps us stay grounded in the present moment, fostering clarity and empathy, while self-care allows us to recharge and approach the world with a refreshed perspective.

Meaningful dialogue is the antidote to misunderstanding and conflict. Engaging in constructive conversations with those who hold different views encourages us to actively listen, seek understanding, and find common ground. It requires us to set aside judgment and ego, approaching these discussions with an open heart and a genuine desire to connect. Through dialogue, we can build bridges of empathy and create spaces for healing and reconciliation.

Cultural diversity is one of humanity's greatest treasures, enriching our lives with a kaleidoscope of colors, languages, and traditions. Yet, cultural differences can also breed misunderstanding and prejudice. Embracing cultural diversity involves celebrating the unique contributions of each culture, acknowledging the hardships they have faced, and seeking to learn from their wisdom. By fostering intercultural understanding, we create a more inclusive and harmonious world where each thread in the tapestry of humanity is cherished.

Amidst the challenges, triumphs emerge when we consciously choose empathy and understanding over judgment and division. Each act of kindness, each moment of genuine connection, and each instance of open-mindedness brings us closer to the realization of a world united by compassion. Triumph lies in the transformation of ourselves and others, as we witness the breaking down of barriers and the building of bridges that transcend differences.

The journey of non-judgment is a perpetual quest, filled with challenges and triumphs that shape us as individuals and as a society. As we navigate the complexities of a diverse world, we must remain steadfast in our commitment to empathy, understanding, and acceptance. By recognizing and challenging our biases, engaging in meaningful dialogue, celebrating cultural diversity, and practicing self-care, we pave the way for a more compassionate and interconnected world. Each step we take towards non-judgment is a step towards weaving a tapestry of unity, where the beauty of our differences and the power of our shared humanity are embraced and celebrated. As we continue this journey, may we be guided by the light of empathy, leading us towards a future where non-judgment is the foundation upon which we build a more harmonious and loving world.

Connection Through Compassion

Compassion is the key to breaking free from judgment. This chapter delves into the transformative power of compassion, its connection to spirituality, and how it fosters a deeper sense of interconnectedness with all people.

God is love. Throughout the ages, the figure of Jesus Christ has remained an unparalleled symbol of love, compassion, and selflessness. His life and teachings have left an indelible mark on humanity, offering a timeless example of how one can live a life driven by empathy and care for others. From healing the sick to comforting the brokenhearted, Jesus consistently displayed a remarkable capacity to be moved with compassion for everyone he encountered. In this chapter, we delve into the instances where the boundless compassion of Jesus shone through, leaving a lasting legacy that continues to inspire and uplift hearts across generations.

In the Gospels, we find a poignant account of a man afflicted with leprosy who approached Jesus, seeking healing and mercy (Matthew 8:1-4). Leprosy was considered one of the most dreaded diseases during that time, and those afflicted were often ostracized from society. Moved with compassion, Jesus not only touched the leper, which was a profound act of breaking societal norms, but also cured him, restoring the man's dignity and reuniting him with his community. In this simple yet profound gesture, Jesus demonstrated that no one was beyond the reach of his love and compassion.

In another extraordinary display of compassion, Jesus came across a multitude of people who had followed him, hungry and tired (Mark 6:30-44). Rather than sending them away, Jesus was deeply moved by their plight and decided to feed them with the meager resources at hand. With only five loaves of bread and two fish, he miraculously multiplied the food, satisfying the hunger of thousands. This act of compassion highlights Jesus' concern for the basic needs of humanity, exemplifying his boundless care for even the most trivial of worries.

The story of the woman caught in adultery (John 8:1-11) reveals Jesus' compassionate response to a woman who faced the risk of stoning, as prescribed by the law. Instead of condemning her, Jesus defended her, challenging her accusers to examine their own hearts. He offered forgiveness and a fresh start, illustrating that compassion transcends judgment, and mercy triumphs over condemnation. This act reflects Jesus' profound love for the broken and downtrodden, emphasizing the importance of offering grace and understanding to those who stumble.

Throughout his ministry, Jesus healed numerous individuals suffering from blindness, lameness, and other disabilities (Matthew 9:27-30, Mark 2:1-12). In each instance, he was moved with compassion for their suffering and responded with miraculous healing. These acts serve as a powerful reminder that Jesus was deeply attuned to the pain and struggles of those around him, and his compassion knew no bounds when it came to alleviating their suffering.

The account of Lazarus' resurrection (John 11:1-44) is a profound testament to the depth of Jesus' compassion. When faced with the grief of Mary and Martha over the death of their brother, Jesus was moved to tears, even though he knew he would raise Lazarus from the dead. This profound act of empathy showcases Jesus' understanding of the human experience and his willingness to share in the pain of others.

The life of Jesus Christ stands as an extraordinary testament to the power of compassion. Time and again, he showed that love and empathy were at the core of his teachings and actions. Whether it was healing the sick, feeding the hungry, defending the oppressed, or raising the dead, Jesus' compassion knew no bounds. His example continues to challenge us to see beyond our differences, embrace our shared humanity, and extend a helping hand to those in need.

In a world often defined by division and strife, the compassion of Jesus serves as a timeless beacon, guiding us toward a more inclusive, understanding, and loving society. May we strive to emulate his boundless compassion, extending kindness to all, and leaving a legacy of love that endures for generations to come.

Jesus' lack of judgment for others was undoubtedly one of the key factors that fueled his boundless compassion. Throughout his teachings, he emphasized the importance of showing love and compassion to all, irrespective of their background, status, or past mistakes. This non-judgmental approach was foundational to his ministry, and it resonated deeply with the people he encountered.

Jesus was known for reaching out to those on the fringes of society - the outcasts, the sinners, and the despised. He was often criticized by the religious leaders of his time for associating with tax collectors, prostitutes, and other "sinners" (Matthew 9:10-13). Yet, his response was clear: he came not to condemn, but to offer redemption and healing. Jesus saw beyond people's actions and recognized the inherent worth in each person, embracing them with open arms and demonstrating a profound lack of judgment.

In one of his most famous parables (Luke 15:11-32), Jesus illustrated the Father's unconditional love and lack of judgment for his wayward son. When the younger son returned home after squandering his inheritance, he expected to be met with anger and rejection. Instead, he was welcomed with open arms and celebrated. This parable exemplifies Jesus' message of God's unfailing love and forgiveness, highlighting his desire for humanity to emulate this unconditional love in their own lives.

The encounter with the Samaritan woman at the well (John 4:1-30) serves as a powerful illustration of Jesus' lack of judgment. As a Jew, Jesus was expected to avoid contact with Samaritans due to historical animosities between the two groups. However, Jesus engaged the woman in a meaningful conversation, acknowledging her as a fellow human being in need of living water - a spiritual thirst that only he could quench. In doing so, he transcended social barriers and displayed compassion without judgment.

In another parable (Luke 18:9-14), Jesus contrasted the attitudes of a self-righteous Pharisee and a humble tax collector. The Pharisee arrogantly judged and looked down upon the tax collector, while the tax collector humbly acknowledged his need for mercy and forgiveness. Jesus commended the latter's attitude, teaching the importance of humility and a lack of judgment when dealing with others.

Perhaps one of the most powerful examples of Jesus' lack of judgment is found in the story of the woman caught in adultery (John 8:1-11). When the scribes and Pharisees brought her before Jesus, ready to stone her, he responded with the famous words, "Let him who is without sin among you be the first to throw a stone at her." Jesus' statement emphasized that none of us are without fault and that we should not be quick to condemn others.

The profound lack of judgment displayed by Jesus Christ was instrumental in his ability to be moved with compassion for everyone. By recognizing the humanity and inherent worth of each individual, he offered a radical message of love, acceptance, and forgiveness. In doing so, Jesus challenged the prevailing norms of his time and continues to inspire people today to embrace compassion and reject judgment.

As we contemplate the life of Jesus and his compassion for humanity, we are compelled to reflect on our own attitudes and actions towards others. Jesus' example challenges us to strive for greater understanding, empathy, and love in our relationships with those around us. By following his lead and embracing a non-judgmental stance, we can sow the seeds of compassion in our communities and contribute to a more compassionate and inclusive world.

In the story of the woman caught in adultery, as mentioned in John 8:1-11, Jesus demonstrates his lack of judgment and compassion in a powerful and transformative way:

Verses 2-5 (NIV):

2 At dawn, he appeared again in the temple courts, where all the people gathered around him, and he sat down to teach them. 3 The teachers of the law and the Pharisees brought in a woman caught in adultery. They made her stand before the group 4 and said to Jesus, "Teacher, this woman was caught in the act of adultery. 5 In the Law, Moses commanded us to stone such women. Now, what do you say?"

The religious leaders were trying to trap Jesus into making a judgment that would contradict the law of Moses. They presented the woman's sin in a public and humiliating manner, expecting Jesus to condemn her.

Verses 6-9 (NIV):

6 They were using this question as a trap, in order to have a basis for accusing him. But Jesus bent down and started to write on the ground with his finger. 7 When they kept on questioning him, he straightened up and said to them, "Let any one of you who is without sin be the first to throw a stone at her." 8 Again he stooped down and wrote on the ground. 9 At this, those who heard began to go away one at a time, the older ones first, until only Jesus was left, with the woman still standing there.

In this moment, Jesus responds to their challenge with profound wisdom and grace. Instead of passing judgment on the woman, he challenges the crowd's conscience by inviting the one without sin to cast the first stone. By doing so,

Jesus reminds them of their own imperfections and the need for humility and self-reflection.

Verses 10-11 (NIV):

10 Jesus straightened up and asked her, "Woman, where are they? Has no one condemned you?" 11 "No one, sir," she said. "Then neither do I condemn you," Jesus declared. "Go now and leave your life of sin."

In this final part of the story, Jesus reveals the depth of his compassion. He acknowledges that no one in the crowd has the right to condemn the woman, and since he, as the sinless Son of God, does not condemn her either, he grants her forgiveness and a fresh start. However, he also gently encourages her to leave her life of sin, showing that compassion doesn't mean overlooking wrongdoing, but rather, it involves guiding and inspiring others to change their ways for the better.

This powerful encounter between Jesus and the woman caught in adultery encapsulates his approach to compassion and non-judgment. Rather than condemning and shaming, Jesus offered understanding, forgiveness, and the opportunity for transformation. This episode serves as a timeless reminder of the importance of showing love and compassion to all, regardless of their past mistakes or shortcomings, and it challenges us to adopt a similar approach in our own interactions with others.

When there is no judgment, there is compassion - this profound truth is at the heart of Jesus' teachings and actions. His lack of judgment paved the way for boundless compassion to flow freely to all, fostering an environment of acceptance, healing, and love.

In his ministry, Jesus encountered many individuals burdened by emotional pain, shame, and guilt. Whether it was the woman caught in adultery, the tax collectors despised by society, or the lepers rejected and isolated, Jesus showed compassion without judgment. Instead of adding to their pain with harsh words or condemnation, he offered healing and restoration. By extending love and understanding, Jesus brought hope to those who felt broken and abandoned, demonstrating that compassion holds the power to mend even the most wounded souls.

The parable of the Good Samaritan (Luke 10:25-37) further exemplifies Jesus' teachings on compassion without judgment. When a man was left half-dead on the roadside, religious figures passed him by, unwilling to help. However, a despised Samaritan, despite being culturally rejected, stopped to aid the injured man. Jesus used this story to illustrate that true compassion transcends societal barriers and is not hindered by prejudices or judgments. He taught that compassion should be extended to all, regardless of race, ethnicity, or social status.

Jesus often displayed a special tenderness toward children. In Mark 10:13-16, when people were bringing children to him, the disciples rebuked them, seeing them as an inconvenience. However, Jesus responded with compassion, stating, "Let the little children come to me, and do not hinder them, for the kingdom of God belongs to such as these." Here, Jesus emphasizes the value of every individual, regardless of age, and showcases his unconditional love and acceptance, devoid of judgment or exclusion.

In Luke 15:1-7, Jesus tells the parable of the lost sheep, highlighting the depth of his compassion for those who have strayed. He describes a shepherd who leaves the ninety-nine sheep to search for the one that wandered off. When he finds it, he joyfully carries it back, emphasizing the value of each soul to God. Jesus teaches that he is the compassionate shepherd who seeks out those who are lost, gently guiding them back into the fold without judgment or reproach.

One of the most profound expressions of Jesus' compassion without judgment is seen during his crucifixion. In the midst of agony and suffering, he prays for his executioners, saying, "Father, forgive them, for they do not know what they are doing" (Luke 23:34). Even in his darkest hour, Jesus exemplifies a heart full of compassion and forgiveness, refusing to condemn those who were responsible for his pain. His sacrificial act on the cross embodies the epitome of compassion, as he willingly gave his life to reconcile humanity with God.

The life and teachings of Jesus Christ exemplify that where there is no judgment, there is compassion. He provided a powerful and transformative model of embracing all individuals, regardless of their background, actions, or mistakes. Through his boundless love and understanding, Jesus showed that compassion has the potential to heal wounds, mend brokenness, and bridge divides. As followers of his example, we are challenged to extend compassion to those around us, recognizing the inherent worth of every person and offering a hand of understanding, forgiveness, and empathy. By doing so, we continue the legacy of compassion that Jesus left behind, transforming lives and radiating love in a world that yearns for such grace and acceptance.

The Mirror Effect

Judgment often reflects our internal struggles and unresolved issues. This chapter explores how judgment can be a mirror reflecting our unmet needs, fears, and insecurities.

In our complex and interconnected world, it's nearly impossible to escape the web of judgment that seems to ensnare us at every turn. Whether we are on the giving or receiving end, judgments are woven into the fabric of human interaction. But have you ever paused to reflect on the root cause of these judgments? Beneath the surface of our seemingly objective assessments of others lies a profound truth: the judgments we cast upon others are often a reflection of our own innate insecurities.

The human mind is a multifaceted labyrinth, intricately woven with emotions, experiences, and beliefs. At the heart of this intricate maze lie our insecurities - those deeply ingrained fears and doubts about our self-worth and capabilities. Unbeknownst to us, these insecurities often find an escape route through the mechanisms of projection. When we encounter traits, behaviors, or qualities in others that remind us of our own fears and inadequacies, we instinctively project these insecurities onto them. By doing so, we temporarily free ourselves from facing our inner demons, even if only at the cost of perpetuating a cycle of judgment and criticism.

The ego, that delicate guardian of our self-identity, seeks to maintain a sense of control and significance. Our insecurities threaten this sense of stability, causing the ego to construct elaborate defense mechanisms to safeguard our self-esteem. One such mechanism is projection, where the ego cunningly redirects attention away from our weaknesses by highlighting the perceived flaws of others.

Imagine encountering a person who exhibits remarkable confidence and charisma, traits you wish to possess but feel you lack. In such a scenario, your ego may respond by criticizing the person as arrogant or fake, subtly diminishing their qualities to protect itself from the discomfort of inadequacy. The irony is that the judgments we cast to shield our egos may very well be masking the qualities we desire most in ourselves.

Our judgments of others are further shaped by our selective perception, influenced by the cognitive biases that color our world. Confirmation bias, for instance, causes us to favor information that aligns with our preexisting beliefs. When we harbor insecurities about our abilities, appearances, or social standing, we tend to unconsciously select information that confirms those insecurities. This perpetuates the cycle of judgment, as we continually find evidence to validate our negative perceptions of both ourselves and others.

Society, as a collective entity, plays a significant role in shaping our perceptions and judgments. Cultural norms, media representation, and societal expectations create a standardized blueprint against which we measure ourselves and others. Insecurities may arise when we feel we don't fit neatly into these molds, prompting us to project those insecurities onto those who challenge societal norms.

For instance, a society that places a high premium on physical appearance may breed insecurity in those who feel they don't conform to the idealized standards. When confronted with someone who defies these standards, their judgment may be a way of deflecting attention from their own perceived shortcomings.

The first step towards breaking free from the vicious cycle of judgment is self-awareness. By introspecting and acknowledging our insecurities, we begin to untangle the web of projection that influences our perceptions of others. Understanding that judgments are often rooted in our own fears can lead to greater compassion and empathy towards those we encounter.

Engaging in honest self-reflection can help us recognize the patterns of projection and discrimination in our thoughts and behaviors. Rather than hastily judging someone, we can take a moment to pause and ask ourselves: "Why does this person trigger such a reaction in me? What insecurities might I be projecting onto them?"

In doing so, we open the door to personal growth and transformation. By addressing our own insecurities, we create space for greater understanding and acceptance of both ourselves and others. Embracing our vulnerabilities not only empowers us to cultivate a healthier self-image but also allows us to see the shared humanity in everyone we encounter.

The recognition that judgment of others is rooted in our own innate insecurities liberates us from the heavy burden of negativity. As we journey through life, let us remember that each judgment cast is an opportunity for self-exploration and growth. By choosing empathy and understanding over prejudice and criticism, we not only uplift others but also embark on a path towards a more compassionate and harmonious world. Embrace your insecurities, for in doing so, you set the stage for profound personal transformation and the dawn of authentic connections with those around you.

In the pursuit of breaking free from the chains of judgment, cultivating empathy and compassion becomes paramount. Empathy is the ability to understand and share the feelings of another, while compassion involves recognizing suffering in others and being motivated to alleviate it. Both qualities are essential in fostering meaningful connections and creating a more tolerant and understanding society.

Empathetic listening is a skill that allows us to truly hear and understand the perspectives and experiences of others without imposing our own judgments. It involves being fully present, setting aside preconceived notions, and creating a safe space for open communication. When we listen with empathy, we become more attuned to the emotions and vulnerabilities of those around us, enabling us to connect on a deeper level.

Imagine encountering someone who behaves aggressively, leading you to judge them as hostile or aggressive. By practicing empathetic listening, you may come to realize that this person is struggling with personal challenges or past traumas that have influenced their behavior. Understanding their pain allows you to respond with compassion instead of perpetuating the cycle of judgment.

In a world as diverse as ours, encountering individuals with different backgrounds, beliefs, and lifestyles is inevitable. Embracing this diversity rather than judging it fosters an inclusive and accepting society. By recognizing that each person is on their unique journey, shaped by a myriad of factors, we can avoid projecting our insecurities onto them.

An attitude of openness and curiosity toward diversity enables us to appreciate the beauty in individual differences and challenges the homogeneity of our judgments. By celebrating diversity, we can discover new perspectives, ideas, and strengths that enrich our lives and broaden our horizons.

In the pursuit of understanding and compassion for others, we must not forget the importance of self-compassion. Acknowledging and accepting our own imperfections with kindness and understanding is crucial in breaking the cycle of projection. When we treat ourselves with compassion, we cultivate a healthier self-image and reduce the need to judge others as a way of deflecting from our insecurities.

Practicing self-compassion involves being gentle with ourselves when we make mistakes, acknowledging our feelings without judgment, and recognizing that we are worthy of love and understanding, just like anyone else. By nurturing self-compassion, we build emotional resilience and gain a more profound capacity for empathy and compassion towards others.

As we strive for empathy and compassion, it is essential to be conscious of societal norms and the role they play in shaping our judgments. By questioning and challenging the stereotypes and biases perpetuated by society, we can break free from the constraints of collective judgments.

Recognizing the impact of societal expectations allows us to understand why certain judgments arise and empowers us to actively combat them. By promoting a culture that embraces diversity, inclusivity, and open-mindedness, we create a ripple effect of empathy that has the potential to transform communities and society at large.

Embracing empathy and compassion is not an instant remedy, but rather a continuous journey of growth and transformation. It requires consistent effort to confront our insecurities, challenge our biases, and actively practice understanding and acceptance. However, the rewards of this journey are profound: a more harmonious inner world, enriched relationships, and a positive impact on the world around us.

As we embark on this path, let us remember that no one is immune to judgment or free from insecurities. By acknowledging this shared vulnerability, we can create a supportive environment where growth and healing are possible for all.

The recognition that judgments of others often stem from our own insecurities opens the door to a new perspective on human interaction. Embracing empathy and compassion transforms our perception of the world, unveiling a deeper understanding of ourselves and others.

By peering into the mirror of our own insecurities, we liberate ourselves from the shadows that cloud our judgments. As we foster empathy and compassion within ourselves, we radiate a guiding light to those around us, illuminating a path toward unity and harmony.

Let us embark on this transformative journey, casting aside the shackles of judgment and embracing the transformative power of empathy. Together, we can co-create a world that nurtures understanding, celebrates diversity, and fosters authentic connections, one compassionate step at a time.

Our insecurities and judgments are deeply entwined, forming a vicious cycle that perpetuates negative thought patterns and behaviors. As we explore this intricate connection, we gain insight into the mechanisms by which our insecurities feed judgment, further solidifying the importance of cultivating empathy and self-awareness.

One of the primary catalysts for judgment is the tendency to compare ourselves to others. In a hyperconnected world driven by social media, comparing our lives, achievements, and appearances to curated versions of others' realities has become all too common. These comparisons inevitably trigger feelings of inadequacy, fueling our insecurities.

When we feel inferior in comparison to someone else, we may attempt to level the playing field by criticizing them. By tearing others down, we momentarily alleviate the burden of our own insecurities, but this relief is fleeting and comes at a high cost – the deterioration of our capacity for empathy and compassion.

Insecurities often lead us to seek validation from external sources, including the approval and praise of others. When we base our self-worth on external validation, we become susceptible to judging others as a means to reinforce our own worthiness.

For example, if we feel insecure about our intelligence, we may seek out opportunities to highlight the shortcomings of others' ideas or opinions. By doing so, we attempt to reaffirm our own intellect and worth in comparison. However, this habit of seeking validation through judgment only deepens the cycle of insecurity, as it further separates us from genuine connections with others.

Projection, as mentioned earlier, plays a pivotal role in how our insecurities manifest as judgments. When we project our fears and inadequacies onto others, we distort our perception of reality and create a distorted lens through which we view the world.

For instance, if we harbor doubts about our abilities in a particular field, we may be more prone to criticize or belittle others who excel in that area. By projecting our insecurities onto them, we shield ourselves from confronting our own limitations, but this defense mechanism comes at the expense of empathy and understanding.

Our judgments can serve as defensive walls, shielding us from potential rejection or vulnerability. When we encounter traits or behaviors that trigger our insecurities, we may resort to judgment as a protective measure. By convincing ourselves that we are superior or that the other person is unworthy, we create a barrier that insulates us from the discomfort of confronting our own vulnerabilities.

For instance, if we feel insecure about our physical appearance, we may subconsciously judge others based on their looks to bolster our own sense of attractiveness. This tactic is an attempt to build an illusion of strength and superiority, but it further reinforces the walls that separate us from authentic connections and understanding.

As the cycle of insecurity and judgment persists, it leaves a lasting impact on society. The collective judgments of individuals contribute to the perpetuation of harmful stereotypes and social norms. These norms, in turn, perpetuate the insecurities of individuals who feel they must conform to societal expectations to be accepted and valued.

For example, a society that places high value on material wealth may lead individuals to judge and stigmatize those who don't fit the mold of material success. As a result, those who don't meet these standards internalize feelings of inadequacy and perpetuate the cycle of judgment in their interactions with others.

Breaking free from the cycle of insecurity and judgment requires a conscious commitment to self-awareness, empathy, and compassion. By acknowledging our insecurities and their connection to our judgments, we can begin the process of healing and personal growth.

Through introspection and self-reflection, we can identify the triggers that lead to judgment and explore the root causes of our insecurities. By facing these fears head-on, we diminish their power to dictate our thoughts and behaviors, enabling us to respond to others with understanding and kindness.

Cultivating empathy and compassion is a journey that requires patience and perseverance. It involves challenging our preconceived notions, embracing vulnerability, and actively seeking to understand the perspectives of others. As we engage in this transformative process, we not only liberate ourselves from the chains of judgment but also contribute to a more compassionate and empathetic world for all.

In conclusion, the insecurities we carry within ourselves create a complex interplay with our judgments of others. As we break down the walls of judgment and embrace the light of empathy, we pave the way for a more harmonious and understanding society, one in which we can truly celebrate the beauty of our shared humanity. The journey is not without its challenges, but the rewards are immeasurable - for ourselves and for those we encounter along the way. Let us embark on this transformative path together, hand in hand, and unlock the power of empathy to illuminate the world with compassion.

The Art of Empathy

Empathy allows us to step into another's shoes, to see the world from their perspective. We will explore the importance of empathy in cultivating a non-judgmental attitude and how it can bridge the gaps between us, fostering understanding and unity.

In a world often marred by divisions, misunderstandings, and conflicts, there exists an extraordinary force capable of bridging the gaps and healing wounds: empathy. This profound ability to understand and share the feelings of others is not just an innate characteristic but also a skill that can be cultivated and harnessed to bring about positive change in our lives and in society. Through empathy, we can navigate the complexities of human emotions, build meaningful connections, and create a more compassionate world.

Empathy is the ability to put ourselves in another person's shoes, to step outside of our own experiences and perceptions, and genuinely comprehend what someone else is going through. It is more than just sympathy, which involves feeling sorry for someone; empathy delves deeper, allowing us to feel with them, to experience their joys, sorrows, fears, and hopes. By embracing empathy, we open our hearts and minds to a profound level of understanding, accepting the unique journeys of others without judgment.

Science has illuminated the neurological underpinnings of empathy. In our brains, mirror neurons play a crucial role in understanding others' emotions. When we witness someone experiencing joy or pain, these neurons activate, leading us to "mirror" their feelings and allowing us to grasp their emotional state at a subconscious level. This mechanism suggests that empathy is an intrinsic aspect of our humanity, a potential wellspring of connection waiting to be tapped.

At its core, empathy is a force for healing. When someone feels truly heard and understood, their emotional burden becomes lighter. By offering empathic support, we provide a safe space for people to process their emotions, fostering personal growth and resilience. Empathy can serve as a beacon of hope for those navigating hardships, reminding them that they are not alone in their struggles.

One of the primary ways we express empathy is through active listening. When we listen with full attention and genuine curiosity, we communicate our willingness to understand and validate the other person's feelings. Active listening involves not only hearing the words but also discerning the underlying emotions and unspoken messages. By developing this skill, we create a more profound connection with others and strengthen our capacity for empathy.

Empathy is a muscle that can be strengthened through practice. To foster empathy within ourselves, we must first become more self-aware. Understanding our own emotions and biases allows us to navigate the minefield of projecting our feelings onto others. Self-compassion, too, is vital, as it enables us to be kinder to ourselves and, in turn, extend that kindness to others.

Teaching empathy to others, particularly the younger generation, is instrumental in shaping a more compassionate world. Education systems can incorporate empathy-building activities, encouraging children to listen to each other, share experiences, and acknowledge diverse perspectives. Modeling empathic behavior in our families, workplaces, and communities sets a powerful example for others to follow.

When conflicts arise, empathy can serve as a potent tool for resolution. By understanding the underlying emotions and concerns of all parties involved, we can foster an atmosphere of mutual respect and compromise. Empathic communication can help dissolve barriers, creating space for open dialogue and constructive problem-solving.

Zooming out to a global scale, empathy holds the potential to bridge the chasm between cultures, nations, and ideologies. By embracing the experiences of others from different backgrounds, we cultivate a sense of unity and interconnectedness. Empathy dissolves the notion of "us" versus "them," instead fostering a collective "we" that recognizes the universal human experience.

While empathy is a powerful force, it is essential to acknowledge its limitations. Feeling the pain of others intensely can be emotionally draining, potentially leading to burnout or compassion fatigue. Balancing empathy with self-care is vital to avoid getting overwhelmed. Moreover, empathy alone cannot solve all the world's problems, but it can inspire actions that drive positive change.

In a world grappling with numerous challenges, empathy stands as a beacon of hope—a force capable of uniting, healing, and transforming lives. By practicing empathy in our daily interactions, we contribute to a ripple effect that radiates beyond ourselves, fostering compassion and understanding in our communities and the world at large. Embracing empathy is not a sign of weakness but of strength, as it allows us to connect on a deeper level, celebrate our shared humanity, and cultivate a more harmonious and compassionate world for generations to come.

Empathy serves as a powerful antidote to the innate human tendency to judge others quickly and harshly. By cultivating a deeper understanding of others' experiences and emotions, empathy dissolves the barriers that prejudice and bias construct. It challenges us to confront our preconceived notions, paving the way for greater acceptance, compassion, and tolerance.

Judgment is a product of human cognition; it arises from our brain's instinct to categorize and make sense of the world around us. While this cognitive process can be helpful in some situations, it can also lead us to oversimplify complex matters and form hasty opinions about people based on limited information or stereotypes. This tendency to judge others often springs from fear, ignorance, or the need to validate our own beliefs and values.

Empathy prompts us to challenge our assumptions and biases. When we actively listen to someone's story, we gain insights into their unique experiences, struggles, and aspirations. We begin to understand that behind their actions and behaviors lie complex webs of circumstances and emotions, often invisible at first glance.

For instance, instead of judging a person who seems aloof or unfriendly, empathy encourages us to consider that they might be going through a difficult time, dealing with anxiety, or facing personal challenges. By resisting snap judgments, we allow room for understanding, realizing that we too are imperfect and can be misunderstood.

Cultivating empathy involves a conscious effort to suspend judgment and genuinely engage with others. Practicing active listening, as discussed earlier, is a crucial component of this process. By putting aside our own agendas and truly focusing on the other person's perspective, we become more receptive to their emotions and experiences.

Additionally, seeking diverse perspectives and exposing ourselves to different cultures, backgrounds, and life stories broadens our empathy. Reading books, watching documentaries, and engaging in open conversations with people from various walks of life expands our worldview, making us less inclined to judge others based on limited knowledge.

Empathy is closely tied to emotional intelligence, the ability to recognize, understand, and manage one's emotions and those of others. As we strengthen our empathy, our emotional intelligence flourishes, leading to greater self-awareness and social awareness.

Through empathy, we become attuned to the emotional cues and nonverbal communication of others, which helps us grasp their underlying feelings and intentions. This heightened emotional intelligence makes us less prone to misinterpretation and judgment, allowing us to navigate social interactions with greater sensitivity and insight.

Empathy breaks down the barriers that separate us from one another. When we approach others with an empathic mindset, we create an atmosphere of trust and openness. People feel validated and understood, enabling them to lower their guard and share their vulnerabilities without fear of judgment.

In this non-judgmental space, genuine connections can flourish. Empathy builds bridges between people from diverse backgrounds and ideologies, fostering an environment where meaningful dialogues and collaborations can occur.

As we embrace empathy and lessen our propensity to judge, we set an example for those around us. Our actions ripple outward, inspiring others to question their biases and prejudices. Empathy begets empathy, creating a chain reaction of understanding and acceptance that can lead to positive societal change.

In a world where judgment and divisiveness often dominate, empathy offers a compelling alternative. By cultivating empathy within ourselves and encouraging it in others, we break free from the shackles of prejudice and ignorance. Empathy allows us to see beyond the surface, embrace the complexities of the human experience, and celebrate the rich tapestry of diverse perspectives.

As we navigate the waters of empathy, we become beacons of compassion, tolerance, and acceptance. In this collective journey, we can envision a world where empathy takes center stage, and judgment recedes into the shadows. Empathy is a transformative force, empowering us to build a more harmonious and understanding world, one heartfelt connection at a time.

In the realm of conflict resolution, empathy stands as a key instrument for fostering understanding, empathy, and reconciliation. When conflicts arise, whether on a personal level or between nations, empathy serves as a powerful catalyst for de-escalation and healing.

When conflicts arise, emotions run high, and it becomes all too easy to entrench ourselves in our positions, vilifying the other side. However, empathy challenges us to step back from our convictions temporarily and view the situation from the perspective of the other party. By doing so, we gain insight into their concerns, fears, and desires, humanizing them beyond their roles as adversaries.

Empathy creates a safe space for both parties to express their emotions openly and honestly. When we empathize with the emotions driving someone's actions, we pave the way for open communication and dialogue. As a result, the potential for miscommunication, escalation, and misunderstanding decreases, increasing the likelihood of finding common ground and mutual solutions.

Incorporating empathy into conflict resolution requires intentional effort from all parties involved. It is crucial to listen actively and non-judgmentally, without interrupting or preparing counterarguments. Acknowledging emotions, even when we don't agree with them, helps establish trust and creates an environment where vulnerability is accepted.

A vital aspect of building empathy in conflict resolution is practicing empathy within ourselves. By understanding our own emotions, motivations, and biases, we develop the capacity to empathize with others more effectively. Self-awareness enables us to approach conflicts with humility, recognizing that we, too, are subject to human fallibility.

Empathic dialogue serves as the cornerstone of conflict resolution. Rather than entering discussions with the intention of proving the other party wrong, empathic dialogue focuses on seeking understanding and common ground. It involves asking open-ended questions and actively listening to the answers, with a genuine desire to comprehend the other's perspective fully.

Through empathic dialogue, we reframe conflicts from "you versus me" to "us versus the problem." This shift in mindset encourages collaborative problem-solving, fostering a sense of unity and shared purpose. As empathy guides us toward a deeper understanding of the other side's needs and concerns, we become better equipped to craft win-win solutions that address the underlying issues comprehensively.

On a broader scale, empathy plays a crucial role in building lasting peace between nations and communities grappling with historical animosities and entrenched conflicts. The process of reconciliation often requires acknowledging past injustices, empathizing with the suffering of those affected, and promoting healing and understanding.

Truth and reconciliation processes, which have been employed in various regions around the world, rely on empathy to facilitate healing and forgiveness. By hearing and acknowledging the stories of those who have suffered, empathic bridges are formed, fostering an environment where empathy supersedes animosity.

Empathy is also an essential catalyst for promoting social change. When we empathize with individuals and communities facing systemic inequalities and injustices, we are compelled to take action to address these issues. Empathy motivates us to stand in solidarity with those facing adversity and work collectively to create a fairer and more equitable world.

Empathy, in its essence, is a transformative force that can mend relationships, bridge divides, and foster peace. It compels us to set aside judgment and embrace understanding, celebrating the richness of human experiences and emotions. By nurturing empathy within ourselves and weaving it into the fabric of our societies, we unlock its full potential to heal wounds, dissolve conflicts, and build a world where compassion and understanding prevail.

As we embark on this empathic journey, let us remember that empathy is not merely a fleeting sentiment but an enduring commitment to treat others with kindness, respect, and love. Through empathy, we can elevate ourselves and humanity as a whole, ensuring that our interactions and decisions are guided by the transformative power of understanding and compassion.

Freedom From Labels

Labels limit our understanding of others and reinforce judgment. In this chapter, we discuss the significance of letting go of preconceived notions, stereotypes, and assumptions, empowering us to see the uniqueness and complexity of each individual.

In a world that thrives on categorization and identification, the practice of labeling others has become an inherent part of human interaction. Labels serve as a shortcut for understanding and processing information about others, helping us make sense of the complex world around us. However, beneath the surface, lies a hidden danger in this seemingly innocent practice of assigning labels to individuals. This chapter explores the dangers of labeling people, shedding light on the negative consequences it can have on both the labeled and the labeler.

Labels can be powerful tools; they provide a sense of identity, belonging, and purpose. They can empower individuals, helping them embrace their strengths and unique qualities. For instance, someone labeled as an "artist" may find confidence and validation in their creative pursuits. On the other hand, labels can also create constraints and limitations, stifle personal growth, and perpetuate stereotypes.

One of the gravest dangers of labeling others is the perpetuation of stereotypes. Labels often simplify complex individuals, reducing them to a single characteristic or trait. Such oversimplification leads to harmful generalizations that can perpetuate prejudice, discrimination, and bias. For example, assigning a label like "lazy" to an individual might overlook the various factors influencing their behavior, such as personal circumstances or mental health issues.

Labels can act as self-fulfilling prophecies, influencing a person's behavior and actions. When individuals are repeatedly labeled in a particular way, they may start internalizing these labels, altering their self-perception and adopting the associated behaviors. For instance, if someone is consistently labeled as "troublemaker," they may begin to believe it and act out in ways that reinforce this perception.

The act of labeling others can also have a profound impact on their mental health. Negative labels can lead to feelings of shame, worthlessness, and isolation, which may contribute to anxiety, depression, or even suicidal thoughts. In contrast, overly positive labels, while seemingly harmless, can create immense pressure and anxiety to live up to unrealistic expectations.

Labels can act as confining boxes, limiting a person's potential for growth and change. When individuals are labeled, they might feel constrained to conform to societal expectations associated with that label, rather than exploring other aspects of their identity or pursuing new opportunities. For instance, someone labeled as "shy" might resist taking on leadership roles or participating in social events, hindering their personal development.

Labeling others often creates divisions among people. It fosters an "us vs. them" mentality, leading to a sense of separation and conflict. These divisions can perpetuate prejudices and animosities between different groups, hindering social cohesion and empathy.

The dangers of labeling others cannot be understated. While labels can offer a semblance of understanding and a sense of identity, they also possess the potential to perpetuate stereotypes, hinder personal growth, and negatively impact mental health. Recognizing the harm that labeling can cause is essential in fostering a more compassionate and inclusive society.

As individuals, we must challenge our tendency to assign labels hastily, seeking instead to understand the complexity and uniqueness of each person we encounter. By embracing the diversity of human experience and avoiding the pitfalls of labeling, we can forge deeper connections, nurture personal growth, and build a more harmonious world for everyone.

In the quest to understand the dangers of labeling others, it is imperative to explore the alternative approach of embracing the complexity of human identity. Recognizing the multifaceted nature of individuals can lead to a more compassionate and empathetic society. This chapter delves into the benefits of adopting a nuanced perspective and highlights the positive impact it can have on our relationships and communities.

Human beings are not one-dimensional entities defined by a single label. Instead, each individual embodies a spectrum of characteristics, experiences, and emotions that shape their identity. Embracing this spectrum allows us to see people beyond mere labels, acknowledging their unique stories and struggles.

Shunning labeling and choosing empathy allows us to put ourselves in someone else's shoes, fostering a deeper understanding of their experiences. By recognizing the diversity of human experiences, we become more tolerant, accepting, and supportive of others, irrespective of their differences.

Labeling can lead to judgment and assumption, often resulting in miscommunication and conflict. Embracing complexity encourages open dialogue, where individuals are more willing to share their thoughts, feelings, and vulnerabilities. This promotes mutual respect and understanding, building bridges rather than walls between people.

Labeling can be influenced by unconscious biases we hold, stemming from our upbringing, culture, and experiences. By acknowledging these biases and actively seeking to challenge them, we can develop a more inclusive mindset that values diversity and rejects harmful stereotypes.

A person's behavior cannot be fully understood without considering the context of their lives. External factors such as upbringing, environment, and socioeconomic status all play a crucial role in shaping an individual's actions and decisions. By considering the broader context, we move away from narrow judgments based on labels and develop a deeper understanding of human behavior.

When we avoid labeling others, we create an environment that encourages growth and change. People are more likely to feel accepted and supported in their journey of self-improvement when they are not confined by limiting labels. As a result, individuals are empowered to embrace new challenges, take risks, and evolve into their best selves.

The journey to abandon labeling others is not an easy one. It requires self-awareness, humility, and a willingness to challenge our preconceived notions continually. However, the rewards of such an endeavor are immeasurable. Embracing the complexity of human identity leads to a society built on compassion, empathy, and understanding.

Let us strive to see beyond labels and appreciate the beauty of diversity in all its forms. By fostering an environment where individuals are valued for their uniqueness and are free from the constraints of limiting labels, we can create a world that celebrates the rich tapestry of human experience. In doing so, we can build stronger communities, cultivate genuine connections, and pave the way for a brighter, more inclusive future for all.

In our current society, labeling others has become deeply ingrained in our collective psyche, perpetuated by programmed biases that often go unnoticed. These biases influence our thoughts, perceptions, and behaviors, leading to the unconscious labeling of individuals based on various attributes. This chapter explores the origins and manifestations of these programmed biases, shedding light on the importance of challenging and dismantling them to foster a more equitable and just society.

From an early age, we are exposed to societal norms, media portrayals, and cultural representations that reinforce certain stereotypes and archetypes. These preconceived notions shape our understanding of various groups, leading to the automatic application of labels based on race, gender, ethnicity, religion, and more. For example, media representations of certain ethnicities as criminals or specific genders as caregivers can perpetuate harmful stereotypes.

Confirmation bias is a cognitive tendency to favor information that confirms our existing beliefs and preconceptions while ignoring or dismissing conflicting evidence. This bias can lead us to label others based on limited or skewed information that supports our preconceived notions, reinforcing existing stereotypes and prejudices.

Humans have a natural inclination to favor individuals from their own "in-group" (those they identify with) and to exhibit bias against individuals from "out-groups" (those perceived as different). This bias can lead to the labeling of out-group members in negative and dehumanizing ways, exacerbating social divisions and reinforcing discriminatory attitudes.

The media plays a significant role in shaping our perceptions and attitudes towards various groups. Biased language and portrayals in news, entertainment, and social media can influence how we label others, either consciously or subconsciously. For example, the use of terms like "illegal immigrant" can stigmatize and dehumanize individuals seeking better opportunities in a new country.

The availability heuristic is a mental shortcut where people rely on readily available information to make judgments or decisions. When we encounter a particular label associated with a group, it becomes more accessible in our minds, leading to the tendency to apply that label to individuals without considering the nuances of their unique identity.

Labeling others can also be influenced by historical prejudices and cultural norms. Deep-rooted biases passed down through generations can shape our perceptions of various groups, influencing the labels we assign to them, and perpetuating systemic discrimination.

Understanding the programmed biases behind labeling is essential in our pursuit of a more inclusive and compassionate society. By acknowledging these biases and actively challenging them, we can break free from the limitations imposed by labels and begin to see individuals as unique human beings deserving of respect and understanding.

As individuals, we can start by examining our own thoughts and behaviors, questioning the labels we apply to others, and seeking to replace them with a more nuanced and empathetic understanding. On a broader scale, we must advocate for diverse and inclusive representations in the media, education, and public discourse to dismantle the harmful stereotypes perpetuated by societal programming.

By embracing complexity, empathy, and a commitment to unlearning programmed biases, we can create a society that values and celebrates the richness of human diversity. Let us work together to challenge the preconceived labels that divide us and build a future where every individual is seen, heard, and respected for their true identity.

As we continue our exploration of the dangers of labeling others and the underlying biases that contribute to this practice, it is crucial to identify practical strategies for overcoming labels and fostering a culture of empowerment and understanding. This chapter delves into actionable steps that individuals, communities, and institutions can take to challenge labeling, promote inclusivity, and create a more compassionate world.

The first step in overcoming labeling is developing self-awareness. Reflect on your own biases and preconceived notions. Engage in introspection and question the origins of your beliefs about different groups. Understanding your biases is crucial in dismantling them and approaching others with an open mind.

Recognize and celebrate the diversity within each individual. People are not defined solely by one characteristic or label; they are multifaceted beings with unique experiences and identities. Embrace the concept of intersectionality, understanding how various aspects of a person's identity intersect and influence their experiences.

Practice active listening and empathy when engaging with others. Seek to understand their perspectives, feelings, and experiences without judgment. This fosters a deeper connection and allows for a more nuanced understanding of their identity beyond any labels.

Education is a powerful tool in challenging programmed biases and dispelling stereotypes. Engage in learning about different cultures, histories, and experiences. Share this knowledge with others to promote awareness and empathy in your community.

Language shapes our perceptions and can perpetuate biases. Choose inclusive language that respects and honors the identities of others. Avoid derogatory terms and be mindful of using labels that generalize or stigmatize specific groups.

Support media and entertainment that offer authentic and diverse representations of individuals and communities. Challenge harmful stereotypes when you encounter them and advocate for responsible and inclusive storytelling.

Institutions play a crucial role in shaping societal attitudes. Encourage and support the creation of policies and practices that promote diversity, equity, and inclusion. Create spaces where individuals from all backgrounds feel valued and represented.

Encourage opportunities for cross-cultural interaction and dialogue. Building relationships with people from diverse backgrounds fosters understanding and breaks down barriers that lead to labeling.

Use your privilege and platform to advocate for marginalized groups and amplify their voices. Be an ally in the fight against discrimination and injustice.

Encourage individuality and celebrate the unique strengths and contributions of each person. Instead of relying on labels to understand others, focus on getting to know individuals on a personal level.

Overcoming the dangers of labeling others requires collective effort and commitment. By cultivating self-awareness, embracing diversity, practicing empathy, and challenging biases, we can create a culture that empowers individuals rather than limiting them with labels.

It is essential to recognize that change starts with each of us. As individuals, we have the power to influence our communities and institutions positively. By taking these actionable steps and advocating for inclusivity and understanding, we can create a world where labeling others gives way to acknowledging and celebrating the richness of human identity. Let us embrace the complexity of individuals, reject harmful stereotypes, and build a society founded on respect, empathy, and unity.

Cultivating Mindfulness

Mindfulness is the practice of being fully present in the moment. Mindfulness can help us become aware of our judgments as they arise and allow them to dissipate, fostering a deeper sense of acceptance and non-reactivity.

In a world filled with diversity and individuality, it is common for people to form judgments about others based on their appearance, beliefs, or actions. Whether it's on social media, in our workplaces, or within our communities, the tendency to judge others is deeply ingrained in human behavior. However, these judgments often lead to negative consequences, perpetuating stereotypes, and fostering division. Mindfulness, a practice rooted in ancient wisdom and now widely embraced in contemporary psychology, offers a powerful antidote to this harmful behavior. In this chapter, we will explore the importance of mindfulness in overcoming judgment of others and cultivating empathy, compassion, and understanding.

To begin, it is essential to recognize that judgment is a natural human response. It stems from our evolutionary past, where quick judgments about potential threats were essential for survival. However, in today's complex society, this instinctive tendency can cause more harm than good. We often judge others based on superficial aspects such as appearance, race, gender, or cultural background, without truly understanding their unique experiences and perspectives.

Unconscious biases further contribute to this behavior. These biases are mental shortcuts that our brains take to process information quickly.

They are shaped by our upbringing, culture, and personal experiences, leading us to make snap judgments without considering the bigger picture. Mindfulness can help us become aware of these biases and challenge them, leading to a more open and compassionate mindset.

Mindfulness is the practice of being fully present and aware of our thoughts, emotions, and surroundings without judgment. By cultivating mindfulness, we learn to observe our thoughts and feelings as they arise, recognizing them without getting entangled in their stories. This non-judgmental awareness allows us to respond to situations with clarity and compassion, rather than reacting impulsively based on preconceived notions.

Mindfulness practices often involve meditation techniques, breathing exercises, and body awareness, all aimed at grounding us in the present moment. Through regular practice, we develop a heightened sense of self-awareness and emotional regulation, which are vital in countering judgmental tendencies.

One of the key benefits of mindfulness is its role in enhancing empathy. Empathy is the ability to understand and share the feelings of others, putting ourselves in their shoes and seeing the world through their eyes. By mindfully observing our thoughts and emotions, we become more attuned to the experiences of others. Instead of dismissing their struggles or perspectives, we begin to appreciate the complexities of their lives.

Through empathy, we create meaningful connections with people from diverse backgrounds and cultures. This fosters a sense of unity and understanding, breaking down the barriers that judgments often erect between individuals and communities.

Mindfulness not only heightens empathy but also nurtures compassion - the desire to alleviate the suffering of others. When we are mindful, we become aware of our own pain and vulnerabilities, which helps us relate to the struggles of others. This shared human experience drives us to extend a helping hand rather than passing judgment.

Compassion enables us to offer support and understanding to those who may be different from us. It allows us to recognize that everyone faces their battles, and it is not our place to judge the paths they have walked. Instead, we can use mindfulness to respond with kindness and genuine concern for their well-being.

Understanding others is a profound aspect of mindfulness. By mindfully listening to people's stories and experiences, we gain insights into the factors that have shaped their lives. We recognize the influence of social and cultural contexts, upbringing, and personal struggles on their behavior and decisions.

This understanding leads to the dismantling of stereotypes and prejudices. Mindfulness helps us acknowledge that our judgments are based on limited information, and there is always more to someone's story than meets the eye. As we become more accepting and understanding of others, we foster an environment where differences are embraced and celebrated.

Conflicts often arise from misunderstandings and judgments. In heated moments, our instinctive response may be to defend our beliefs and criticize others. Mindfulness, however, allows us to pause before reacting impulsively. It helps us detach from the intense emotions of the situation and respond with clarity and empathy.

When engaging in conflict resolution, mindfulness enables active listening and a willingness to understand opposing viewpoints.

By acknowledging our own biases and being open to change, we create a space for constructive dialogue and compromise.

Mindfulness is a transformative practice that empowers individuals to overcome the harmful habit of judging others. By cultivating empathy, compassion, understanding, and self-awareness, we develop a profound appreciation for the diversity of the human experience. Mindfulness serves as a powerful tool in building bridges between people and fostering harmonious, inclusive communities. As we continue on our mindfulness journey, we contribute to a world where acceptance and kindness prevail over judgment and division.

As we deepen our mindfulness practice, it becomes more than just a meditative exercise; it becomes an integral part of our daily lives. Mindfulness extends beyond formal meditation sessions and permeates into our interactions with others, our work, and even our personal thoughts and emotions.

Mindful communication involves being fully present when listening to others and expressing ourselves authentically. Instead of jumping to conclusions or interrupting, we practice active listening, giving others the space to share their thoughts and emotions without judgment. By choosing our words carefully and considering their impact, we contribute to positive and compassionate conversations.

In professional settings, mindfulness can foster a more inclusive and collaborative environment. When colleagues approach their work with mindfulness, they become more attuned to one another's needs, concerns, and ideas. This leads to enhanced teamwork, reduced conflict, and increased productivity.

Mindfulness also plays a crucial role in decision-making. By approaching choices with non-judgmental awareness, we can recognize any biases that might influence our judgment. This helps us make more objective and compassionate decisions that consider the well-being of all involved parties.

Mindfulness encourages self-reflection, where we honestly examine our own actions, thoughts, and intentions. Through this process, we become more aware of our own judgmental tendencies and work to cultivate greater acceptance and understanding of ourselves and others.

Practicing mindfulness teaches us to accept the imperfections in ourselves and others. Instead of striving for perfection or holding others to unrealistic standards, we learn to appreciate the beauty of our shared humanity, complete with flaws and vulnerabilities. This understanding allows us to let go of the need to judge and criticize, fostering an atmosphere of kindness and self-compassion.

Moreover, mindfulness nurtures a growth mindset, recognizing that people can change and evolve over time. When we approach others with an open mind, we create opportunities for growth and learning, both for ourselves and for those around us. As we release the grip of judgment, we embrace the potential for positive transformation and personal development.

While mindfulness offers numerous benefits in overcoming judgment, the journey is not without challenges. At times, we might catch ourselves slipping into old habits of judgment or becoming overwhelmed by our emotions. However, these challenges are also opportunities for growth and deepening our practice.

During moments of judgment or self-criticism, self-compassion becomes essential. Rather than berating ourselves for our mistakes, we practice self-kindness and understanding. By extending this same compassion to others when they falter, we create a more forgiving and supportive environment.

Mindfulness encourages us to let go of grudges and resentments, acknowledging that holding onto negative emotions only harms ourselves. Forgiveness liberates us from the burden of judgment and allows us to move forward with greater clarity and peace.

Mindfulness is a continuous practice that requires patience and persistence. Changing long-standing habits of judgment takes time and effort, but the rewards are well worth it. As we persist in our mindfulness journey, we cultivate a more compassionate and non-judgmental approach to life.

The importance of mindfulness in overcoming judgment of others cannot be overstated. Mindfulness empowers us to break free from the constraints of bias and preconceived notions, opening our hearts and minds to the vast array of human experiences. By cultivating empathy, compassion, understanding, and self-awareness, we become agents of positive change in our communities and the world.

Mindfulness is not a quick fix but a transformative process that requires ongoing dedication. Through mindful living, we foster authentic connections with others, dissolve the barriers of judgment, and embrace the beauty of our shared humanity. As we continue to embrace mindfulness in our lives, we move toward a more compassionate and harmonious world, where acceptance and understanding triumph over division and judgment. Let us embark on this mindful journey together, supporting one another in our growth and collective endeavor to create a more compassionate and empathetic world.

Central to the practice of mindfulness is cultivating awareness of our thoughts, emotions, and underlying motives. This self-awareness serves as a crucial tool in overcoming judgment of others, as it allows us to recognize when judgmental thoughts arise and understand the reasons behind them. By being aware of our thought patterns and motivations, we can take conscious steps to redirect our minds toward more compassionate and understanding responses.

Our minds constantly produce thoughts, some of which are judgmental in nature. Mindfulness teaches us not to suppress these thoughts, but rather to observe them without attachment or aversion. When we notice judgmental thoughts emerging, we can acknowledge them without judgment and gently guide our attention back to the present moment.

Mindfulness encourages us to explore the underlying motives behind our judgments. Often, judgment arises from fear, insecurity, or feelings of superiority. By honestly examining these motivations, we can begin to dismantle their power over our thoughts and actions.

Self-awareness allows us to recognize moments when we lack empathy and compassion. When we witness ourselves passing judgment on others, we can pause and consider the possible reasons behind their behavior. This opens the door to a more empathetic response, as we remind ourselves that we, too, have flaws and vulnerabilities.

Mindfulness invites us to recognize that our thoughts and emotions are not who we are; they are transient phenomena that come and go. By not identifying with our judgments or letting them define us, we create space for personal growth and transformation.

In challenging situations where judgment might easily arise, mindfulness can be particularly beneficial. By being fully present and aware of our thoughts and motives, we can navigate these moments with greater wisdom and compassion.

When faced with a situation that triggers judgment, taking a mindful pause can be immensely helpful. Instead of reacting impulsively, we can step back, take a few deep breaths, and observe our thoughts and emotions without judgment. This pause allows us to respond more thoughtfully and empathetically.

Mindfulness enables us to see situations from multiple angles, encouraging us to consider alternative perspectives. By adopting a more inclusive view, we become less inclined to make snap judgments and more willing to appreciate the complexities of the human experience.

Judgment often arises from a sense of righteousness or a belief that our opinions are superior to others'. Mindfulness reminds us that no one has a monopoly on truth, and everyone's experiences are valid. Letting go of the need to be right opens us up to greater understanding and harmony.

Mindfulness is not a destination but a journey. As we progress in our practice, we might encounter moments of regression or find ourselves slipping into old patterns of judgment. It is essential to approach these instances with self-compassion and the understanding that change takes time.

Mindfulness encourages us to embrace our imperfections and treat ourselves with the same compassion we extend to others. Acknowledging that we are all on a path of growth helps us maintain a non-judgmental attitude toward ourselves and others.

When we catch ourselves engaging in judgment, it is an opportunity for self-reflection and learning. Rather than chastising ourselves, we can investigate the triggers and underlying emotions that led to the judgment. These insights become valuable lessons for our ongoing journey of mindfulness.

Mindfulness empowers us to be fully present and aware of our thoughts, emotions, and motives. By cultivating this self-awareness, we can overcome the harmful habit of judging others and embrace a more empathetic and compassionate approach to life. By pausing before reacting, examining the roots of our judgments, and practicing self-compassion, we lay the foundation for a transformative journey of growth and understanding.

Mindfulness is not about eliminating judgment altogether, for it is a natural aspect of human cognition. Rather, it is about recognizing judgment when it arises, understanding its impact, and choosing to respond with empathy and kindness. As we continue on this continuous journey of mindfulness, we contribute to a more harmonious and interconnected world, where empathy and understanding transcend the boundaries of judgment and division. Let us walk this path with open hearts and minds, committed to building a brighter future for ourselves and generations to come.

Forgiveness and Letting Go

Forgiveness is a powerful tool for releasing the grip of judgment. This chapter explores the healing nature of forgiveness, both towards others and ourselves and how it liberates us from the burden of holding grudges.

The human heart, with its capacity for compassion, empathy, and love, also bears the burden of judgment. We judge others based on their actions, beliefs, and appearances, often without fully understanding their circumstances or struggles. This chapter explores the profound power of forgiveness in liberating our hearts from the chains of judgment.

Judgment is a natural aspect of the human psyche. It stems from our instinct to make sense of the world and protect ourselves from perceived threats. However, unchecked judgment can lead to prejudice, discrimination, and a closed mind. By examining the roots of our judgments, we can begin to recognize their fallibility and limitations.

To embrace forgiveness, we must cultivate empathy - the ability to put ourselves in another's shoes, to understand their experiences and emotions. Empathy opens the door to compassion, softening our hearts and allowing us to view others as complex individuals with their own struggles and wounds.

Research has shown that forgiveness is not just a moral virtue but also beneficial to our mental and emotional well-being. The act of forgiveness can reduce stress, anxiety, and depression while promoting a sense of inner peace and resilience.

It is a gift we give ourselves as much as to those we forgive.

When we hold onto judgments and grudges, we perpetuate a cycle of pain and resentment. By breaking this cycle through forgiveness, we pave the way for healing and growth. Forgiveness enables us to release the burden of negativity and create space for understanding, reconciliation, and renewal of relationships.

Before we can extend forgiveness to others, we must learn to forgive ourselves. Self-judgment can be one of the most insidious forms of negativity, preventing us from fully embracing our potential and hindering our ability to forgive others genuinely. The journey of self-forgiveness is an essential aspect of releasing judgments of others.

We often expect perfection from ourselves and others, leading to harsh judgments when reality falls short. Embracing forgiveness means acknowledging that imperfection is an intrinsic part of the human experience. We can learn to view mistakes and flaws not as failures but as opportunities for growth and understanding.

Forgiveness does not mean turning a blind eye to harmful actions or excusing wrongdoing. Instead, it involves confronting these actions with empathy and compassion while holding individuals accountable for their behavior. By seeking understanding and encouraging growth, we can transform judgment into a catalyst for positive change.

Throughout history, forgiveness has played a significant role in healing societies, ending conflicts, and fostering reconciliation. Drawing on examples from various cultures and traditions, we explore how forgiveness has been instrumental in creating a better world and promoting social harmony.

Forgiveness is not always easy, and sometimes it feels like an arduous journey filled with inner turmoil and resistance. We delve into the challenges of forgiveness and share stories of individuals who have triumphed over their judgment and found the courage to forgive, inspiring us to undertake this hero's journey ourselves.

The power of forgiveness extends beyond the individual, touching the lives of others in unexpected ways. We explore the ripple effect forgiveness can have on families, communities, and even nations, demonstrating how one act of forgiveness can spark a wave of positive change.

Building a culture of forgiveness requires collective effort and a commitment to empathy, understanding, and acceptance. We discuss practical steps for cultivating forgiveness in our personal lives, communities, and institutions, fostering a more compassionate and interconnected world.

Forgiveness holds the key to releasing the chains of judgment that bind us to negativity and separation. It empowers us to extend grace, understanding, and compassion to ourselves and others, fostering healing, reconciliation, and growth. Embracing forgiveness is not a sign of weakness but a testament to the strength and resilience of the human spirit, leading us toward a brighter and more harmonious future.

The Bible, as one of the most revered and influential religious texts, contains numerous verses and teachings about forgiveness and the importance of releasing judgment of others. Let us delve into some of these profound passages that highlight the power of forgiveness:

Matthew 6:14-15 (New International Version):

"For if you forgive other people when they sin against you, your heavenly Father will also forgive you. But if you do not forgive others their sins, your Father will not forgive your sins."

This passage emphasizes the reciprocity of forgiveness. It reminds us that to receive forgiveness from God, we must also extend forgiveness to others. By doing so, we break the cycle of judgment and embrace a transformative journey towards grace and redemption.

Colossians 3:13 (New Living Translation):

"Make allowance for each other's faults, and forgive anyone who offends you. Remember, the Lord forgave you, so you must forgive others."

The Apostle Paul encourages believers to be compassionate and forgiving towards one another. As recipients of God's forgiveness, we are called to extend that same forgiveness to those who have wronged us. This verse underscores the interconnectedness of forgiveness and how it fosters unity and understanding in relationships.

Luke 6:37 (English Standard Version):

"Judge not, and you will not be judged; condemn not, and you will not be condemned; forgive, and you will be forgiven."

Here, Jesus speaks about the dangers of judgment and the freedom that comes from forgiveness. By releasing the inclination to judge others, we liberate ourselves from the burden of condemnation and open our hearts to the transformative power of forgiveness.

Ephesians 4:31-32 (New International Version):

"Get rid of all bitterness, rage, and anger, brawling and slander, along with every form of malice. Be kind and compassionate to one another, forgiving each other, just as in Christ God forgave you."

In this passage, Paul urges believers to let go of negative emotions and adopt a forgiving spirit. Forgiveness is not only a personal act but also a reflection of Christ's forgiveness towards us. It encourages a shift towards love, compassion, and understanding, breaking the chains of judgment and bitterness.

Mark 11:25 (New King James Version):

"And whenever you stand praying, if you have anything against anyone, forgive him, that your Father in heaven may also forgive you your trespasses."

Jesus emphasizes the significance of forgiveness during prayer. When we approach God with a heart burdened by judgment and unforgiveness, we hinder our spiritual growth. Forgiveness opens the door to God's grace and mercy, fostering a deeper connection with the divine.

Matthew 18:21-22 (New International Version):

"Then Peter came to Jesus and asked, 'Lord, how many times shall I forgive my brother or sister who sins against me? Up to seven times?' Jesus answered, 'I tell you, not seven times, but seventy-seven times.'"

Jesus challenges Peter's understanding of forgiveness by teaching the limitless nature of forgiveness. Forgiving others should not have a set limit but should be a continuous act of grace and love. This radical concept challenges us to break free from the chains of judgment and embrace boundless forgiveness.

These biblical passages convey the transformative power of forgiveness and the necessity of releasing judgment of others. Embracing forgiveness is not only an act of kindness towards those who have wronged us but also an essential aspect of our spiritual growth and relationship with the divine. By following the teachings of forgiveness found in the Bible, we can experience the liberation of our hearts and the healing of our souls.

When we forgive, we release judgment of others, allowing a profound transformation to take place within ourselves. The act of forgiveness is not just an external gesture but a deep internal shift that sets us free from the burden of judgment. Let us explore this concept further and cite additional examples from the Bible that exemplify the connection between forgiveness and the release of judgment:

Romans 14:10 (New International Version):

"You, then, why do you judge your brother or sister? Or why do you treat them with contempt? For we will all stand before God's judgment seat."

In this verse, the Apostle Paul urges believers not to judge or hold contempt for one another. The reminder of God's ultimate judgment encourages us to release our judgments of others and entrust their actions to the divine justice. Forgiveness is an expression of faith in God's sovereignty and understanding that we are not the ultimate judges of others' actions or intentions.

Galatians 5:22-23 (New International Version):

"But the fruit of the Spirit is love, joy, peace, forbearance, kindness, goodness, faithfulness, gentleness, and self-control. Against such things, there is no law."

Forgiveness is an embodiment of the fruits of the Spirit, which include love, peace, and kindness. By practicing forgiveness, we cultivate these virtues within ourselves, leading to a heart free from judgment and filled with compassion and understanding.

Luke 23:34 (New International Version):

"Jesus said, 'Father, forgive them, for they do not know what they are doing.' And they divided up his clothes by casting lots."

Even in the face of great suffering and injustice, Jesus exemplified the power of forgiveness. As he hung on the cross, He forgave those who crucified Him, showing the way to release judgment and embrace mercy and love. This act of forgiveness transcends human understanding and serves as an ultimate example of the transformative power of forgiving others.

Matthew 9:2-7 (New International Version):

"Some men brought to Him a paralyzed man, lying on a mat. When Jesus saw their faith, He said to the man, 'Take heart, son; your sins are forgiven.'... Then He said to the paralyzed man, 'Get up, take your mat and go home.'"

In this powerful story, Jesus forgives the paralyzed man's sins before healing him physically. This illustrates that forgiveness and healing are intrinsically linked. When we release judgment and forgive others, we experience a spiritual and emotional healing that can lead to reconciliation and restoration of broken relationships.

Matthew 5:44 (New International Version):

"But I tell you, love your enemies and pray for those who persecute you."

Jesus challenges His followers to go beyond conventional norms and embrace a higher standard of love and forgiveness. Loving our enemies and praying for those who hurt us allows us to release the chains of judgment and approach difficult situations with grace and compassion.

Forgiveness is a transformative act that goes hand in hand with releasing judgment of others. As we forgive, we open ourselves to the healing power of love and compassion. By looking to the teachings and examples found in the Bible, we can learn to embrace forgiveness as a means to release the burden of judgment, fostering inner peace and deepening our connection with others and with the divine.

The human heart is a delicate canvas that bears the scars of past hurts and traumas. When we hold onto grudges and resentments, we inadvertently lock ourselves in a cycle of pain, preventing the healing process from taking place.

Bitterness is like poison, slowly seeping into every aspect of our lives, affecting our emotional well-being, relationships, and overall happiness. Forgiveness is the antidote that unravels these chains of bitterness. By choosing to forgive, we free ourselves from the clutches of resentment and pave the way for emotional liberation.

Forgiveness is the art of letting go – releasing the grip we have on past hurts and grievances. It is not about condoning the actions of others but about freeing ourselves from the weight of those actions.

In the process of forgiving others, we cultivate compassion - the ability to empathize with the struggles and imperfections of fellow human beings. Compassion becomes the healer, not only for those we forgive but also for ourselves. By extending compassion, we open our hearts to healing and genuine connection with others.

Hurt people often hurt others, perpetuating a cycle of pain and suffering. Forgiveness breaks this cycle, as it disrupts the pattern of retaliation and vengeance. By choosing forgiveness, we become agents of change, promoting healing not only within ourselves but also in the lives of those around us.

Carrying the burden of unforgiveness disrupts our inner peace, causing turmoil and unrest within our souls. This chapter explores how forgiveness is a path to rediscovering inner peace. By making peace with our past and those who have hurt us, we create space for serenity and contentment to flourish in our hearts.

Forgiving others requires us to be vulnerable and acknowledge our pain. Instead of seeing vulnerability as a sign of weakness, we learn to embrace it as an act of courage and strength. This chapter explores how vulnerability through forgiveness empowers us to heal and grow from our experiences.

Before we can fully forgive others, we must extend forgiveness to ourselves. Often, we carry the weight of guilt and shame for our own mistakes and shortcomings. Self-forgiveness is a crucial step in the healing process, enabling us to release self-judgment and embrace self-compassion.

Forgiveness opens the floodgates of emotional liberation. By forgiving others, we release ourselves from the emotional prisons we unknowingly construct.

Forgiveness is a journey of understanding, where empathy becomes the compass guiding us towards healing. As we forgive others, we foster empathy within ourselves, paving the way for deeper connections and compassion towards all beings.

By choosing to forgive others, we open the doors to personal growth, inner healing, and a life lived with love, compassion, and understanding. We acknowledge that forgiveness is not always easy, but the rewards it offers for our well-being and soul's journey make it a powerful and liberating choice.

In the journey of life, forgiveness becomes a transformative path to wholeness. By forgiving others, we heal ourselves. Through forgiveness, we embrace our shared humanity, acknowledging that we are all imperfect beings on this remarkable journey of growth and redemption. As we release judgment and extend compassion, we find the courage to heal and step into the fullness of our authentic selves, embracing the beauty of life and the boundless potential of the human heart.

Embracing Diversity

Embracing diversity is a celebration of the rich tapestry of life. By embracing unity amid our differences, we can foster a more inclusive and loving world.

In the quiet moments of introspection, when we step back from the hustle and bustle of our daily lives, a profound realization dawns upon us – the world is a wondrous tapestry of diversity, intricately woven with threads of existence that bear the mark of the divine. It is in this very diversity that the essence of the divine is expressed, a celestial dance of creation that spans beyond our comprehension.

As we venture into the depths of this divine tapestry, we encounter the myriad forms of life that inhabit this planet. From the towering giants of the ancient forests to the tiniest creatures dwelling in the depths of the oceans, each living being holds a unique space in the grand design of existence. The majestic wings of an eagle, the vivid colors of a butterfly's wings, and the ethereal beauty of blooming flowers – they all serve as a testament to the divine's endless creativity.

Yet, diversity extends far beyond the realm of living organisms. It encompasses the varied landscapes that stretch across continents and the diverse climates that nurture distinct ecosystems. It includes the ever-changing seasons that paint nature's canvas in different hues, a symphony of life that plays out in harmonious rhythm.

In the expanse of the cosmos, too, we find diversity in the myriad celestial bodies that twinkle in the night sky. The majestic stars, the mesmerizing planets, and the celestial phenomena that stir our curiosity – all contribute to the cosmic kaleidoscope, the divine spectacle that invites us to ponder our place in the vastness of space.

When we gaze into the faces of our fellow human beings, we are met with a mosaic of cultures, traditions, and beliefs. From the folklores passed down through generations to the intricate rituals that mark important milestones, each culture reflects a distinct facet of the divine's expression through humanity. Our languages, music, art, and cuisine – all bear the imprints of the divine's touch.

Yet, for all the richness and beauty in diversity, we must acknowledge that it also presents challenges. Misunderstandings, conflicts, and prejudices can arise when we fail to recognize the interconnectedness of all existence. The divine, in its wisdom, has bestowed upon us the gift of free will and individuality, but it is also an invitation to cultivate compassion and empathy towards one another.

To embrace diversity fully, we must acknowledge that our uniqueness and differences do not separate us but rather unite us in a greater tapestry of interconnectedness. Just as each thread in a tapestry plays a crucial role in creating the whole, so does each living being and aspect of creation contribute to the grand design of the universe. It is in recognizing and respecting this interconnectedness that we come closer to understanding the divine's true intention behind such diversity.

In our journey through life, we must strive to be co-creators of harmony and unity. By acknowledging that diversity is the divine expressing itself, we open ourselves to a higher purpose – to celebrate the differences, to learn from one another, and to forge bonds that transcend the boundaries of race, religion, and nationality.

Let us walk hand in hand, guided by the belief that the divine exists within each one of us. With love as our compass, let us navigate the seas of diversity with humility, knowing that the divine's masterpiece lies not just in the stars above but in the hearts of all living beings.

As we traverse this boundless tapestry, may we embrace the oneness that underlies our diverse forms and dance in harmony with the rhythm of the divine expression. In doing so, we honor the brilliance of the universe's design and weave a symphony of unity that resonates with the very heart of creation.

The notion of diversity and uniqueness is deeply ingrained in the very fabric of creation, a reflection of the divine's infinite wisdom and creativity. As we look at the world around us, we find that God intentionally designed each entity with its distinct characteristics, purpose, and role to play in the grand tapestry of existence.

From the vast array of flora and fauna that populate the Earth to the diverse range of geological formations that shape the landscapes, we witness the fingerprints of God in every detail. The Creator's decision to craft such a diverse array of life forms reveals a divine intention to celebrate individuality and highlight the importance of every creature in the cosmic dance.

Consider the human family, for instance. No two individuals are identical; each person possesses a unique blend of physical attributes, talents, and temperaments. This beautiful diversity allows for endless possibilities in relationships, collaborations, and growth. The colors of our skin, the languages we speak, and the cultures we cherish all exemplify God's artistry in celebrating human variation.

As we delve deeper into the wonders of science, we uncover the complexity and diversity within the very building blocks of life – the DNA. God, in His omniscience, fashioned DNA to encode an unfathomable range of genetic traits, ensuring that life would evolve in countless ways across time and space.

Moreover, the ecosystems that thrive on Earth's surface exemplify the delicate balance that God intricately designed. Each species, from the smallest microorganism to the most significant predator, has a specific role in maintaining ecological harmony. The predator-prey relationships, the symbiotic partnerships, and the delicate cycles of life and death all reflect the Creator's ingenious plan.

Even the celestial bodies scattered throughout the cosmos testify to God's love for diversity. The countless galaxies, each containing billions of stars and planets, exhibit the vastness of the divine imagination. In this vastness, there is room for infinite possibilities and an acknowledgment of a universe beyond human comprehension.

Embracing the uniqueness of creation also calls for recognizing the purpose behind these differences. The varied climates that emerge across the globe invite us to adapt and thrive in different conditions. The diverse challenges we face throughout life serve as opportunities for growth, resilience, and compassion. Our distinct backgrounds and experiences encourage us to learn from one another and appreciate the richness that comes from sharing our stories.

Ultimately, it is through embracing diversity and uniqueness that we draw closer to the essence of the divine. In each difference, we glimpse a fragment of God's boundless nature, for the Creator encompasses all facets of existence. By recognizing that God dwells within everything and everyone, we awaken to the unity that underlies this dazzling diversity.

Moreover, the Quran, the Bible, the Bhagavad Gita, and other sacred texts abound with verses that speak to the magnificence of God's diverse creation. These holy scriptures celebrate the uniqueness of every soul and underscore the divine's intention in designing such a multifaceted world.

The world, in all its diversity and uniqueness, is a testament to the divine's multifaceted expression. God's creation reveals itself in the intricate details of life, from the smallest atom to the grandest galaxies. By cherishing this diversity and seeking to understand the purpose behind it, we draw closer to the divine and unveil the interconnectedness that binds us all. As we honor the grand symphony of creation, we acknowledge the divine's profound love and wisdom in granting each being its special place in the tapestry of existence.

Indeed, the beauty of creation lies in the fact that no two individuals are the same – we are all uniquely fashioned by the divine hand. Just as every snowflake boasts its distinctive pattern, each human being possesses a singular blend of qualities that sets them apart. This inherent uniqueness instills a profound significance to every life, illuminating our path with purpose and individuality.

Embracing our individual uniqueness is an act of gratitude to the Creator, for it acknowledges the divine's infinite creativity and love. We are masterpieces of the divine artistry, designed with unparalleled intricacy and care. Our distinct physical features, personalities, and talents form a harmonious symphony, where each note plays an essential role in the grand composition of existence.

While some may perceive our differences as a source of division, embracing our individuality becomes an empowering force that unites us as a human family. Our diversity nurtures an environment of learning, understanding, and respect, fostering a rich cultural exchange that enriches our lives immeasurably. When we engage with others, appreciating their unique perspectives and experiences, we glimpse the myriad ways the divine expresses itself in human form.

Just as a vibrant garden thrives with diverse flowers, the world flourishes through the collective brilliance of its inhabitants. Our differences offer opportunities for collaboration and innovation, allowing us to tackle challenges from diverse angles and develop inclusive solutions that benefit all. When we celebrate and honor our uniqueness, we foster an environment where everyone feels valued, accepted, and embraced for who they are.

Moreover, the acceptance of our individuality leads us to explore the depths of our inner selves, recognizing our potential and purpose in this vast universe. Each soul bears a distinct purpose and journey, and by acknowledging our individual paths, we can find fulfillment and meaning in our lives. In this pursuit of self-discovery, we learn to love ourselves unconditionally and, in turn, extend that love to others.

It is essential to remember that our uniqueness extends beyond the superficial surface of our appearances. The essence of our being – our dreams, aspirations, and beliefs – reflects the infinite diversity of the divine's expression. By nurturing our authentic selves, we can radiate our inner light, becoming beacons of inspiration for others to do the same.

In recognizing our uniqueness, we are also reminded of our interconnectedness. The tapestry of existence is woven together by countless threads, where each life impacts others in profound and often unforeseen ways. Our thoughts, actions, and emotions ripple outward, leaving an indelible mark on the world around us.

As we journey through life, embracing our individuality and honoring that of others, we co-create a world that harmonizes with the divine's intention. The key lies in celebrating diversity without falling prey to judgment or prejudice, for it is the very differences that contribute to the richness of life's experience.

The divine's expression through creation is a testament to the grandeur of diversity and uniqueness. Each life, every soul, carries a spark of the divine, and by embracing our individuality, we discover the true meaning of our existence. Let us celebrate our uniqueness, recognizing that we are all integral parts of the divine masterpiece, united in our diversity, and bound by the sacred thread of existence. In doing so, we honor the divine's wisdom and compassion, and together, we dance to the rhythm of life's ever-unfolding symphony.

When we wholeheartedly embrace the diversity and uniqueness present in the world, it becomes a catalyst for a profound transformation within ourselves. The recognition of the divine expressing itself in countless forms encourages us to shed the shackles of judgment and prejudice, leading us to view one another through the lens of compassion and understanding.

As we immerse ourselves in the rich tapestry of human experience, we come to realize that judgments are merely surface-level assessments that fail to capture the depth and complexity of each individual. Our unique backgrounds, experiences, and struggles shape us into the individuals we are today, and no single judgment can encapsulate the entirety of someone's story.

In the presence of diversity, we discover that our preconceived notions and biases only serve to blind us from the true essence of humanity. These judgments become barriers that impede our ability to connect genuinely with others, preventing us from appreciating the beauty and wisdom they bring to the collective human experience.

Instead, embracing diversity opens our hearts and minds to the vastness of human potential. We begin to see that every individual is a living embodiment of the divine's boundless creativity and love. Just as an artist expresses their emotions through their art, the divine expresses itself through the kaleidoscope of humanity, allowing each of us to shine forth with our own unique brilliance.

Furthermore, our journey toward recognizing the divine in diversity leads us to cultivate empathy – the ability to understand and share the feelings of others. Empathy dismantles the walls that judgments build, as it invites us to step into the shoes of another, see the world through their eyes, and appreciate the struggles they face. In this shared vulnerability, we discover our common humanity, forging connections that bridge the gaps created by judgment.

Through empathy, we learn to listen actively, seeking to understand rather than impose our perspectives. We recognize that every voice, no matter how different from our own, deserves to be heard and acknowledged. This active listening creates a space for dialogue, fostering a culture of inclusion and respect that celebrates diversity rather than fearing it.

Moreover, the absence of judgments grants us the freedom to explore and learn from one another.

We become curious about the wealth of knowledge, traditions, and wisdom that different cultures and backgrounds offer. By embracing diversity, we open ourselves to a lifetime of continuous growth and enrichment, as we absorb the lessons and insights that only a varied world can provide.

As we journey through life, guided by the divine's celebration of diversity, we become ambassadors of love and unity. We recognize that our diversity is not a challenge to overcome but a gift to cherish. Instead of viewing our differences as a source of division, we understand that they are the very threads that weave the fabric of a compassionate and harmonious world.In conclusion, embracing the divine expression of diversity liberates us from the chains of judgment and

prejudice. As we celebrate each individual's uniqueness, we grow in empathy and open-mindedness, seeing the world through a lens of compassion. We become agents of change, breaking down barriers, and building bridges that unite us as one human family. In this celebration of diversity, we embody the essence of the divine, for the ultimate expression of the divine lies in the interconnectedness and oneness of all creation.

A World Transformed

In the final chapter, we will reflect on our transformative journey from judgment to compassion. We will explore the profound impact of our spiritual growth on the world around us and how, by embodying non-judgment, we can inspire positive change and create a more compassionate and harmonious global community.

In the vast tapestry of human existence, few concepts hold as much potential for radical change and growth as the act of releasing judgment. Throughout history, societies have been shaped by a collective inclination to form opinions, make assumptions, and pass judgments on one another. Yet, there lies an untapped well of wisdom and unity that awaits those who dare to free themselves from the shackles of preconceived notions.

Judgment, both subtle and overt, is an integral aspect of the human experience. It arises from our inherent capacity to evaluate and categorize the world around us. From our earliest years, we are taught to discern between right and wrong, good and bad. While such discernment may be essential for personal safety and survival, the consequences of unchecked judgment extend far beyond the individual.

The judgment we cast upon others seldom remains isolated within its intended confines. Rather, it ripples outwards like a stone cast into a still pond, affecting not only the one judged but also those who witness the act. Each judgment made reinforces societal norms and constructs, contributing to the perpetuation of stereotypes, prejudices, and discrimination.

As judgments accumulate, a cycle of separation emerges. People become fragmented into groups defined by arbitrary distinctions, such as race, religion, or social status. Fear and mistrust replace compassion and empathy, widening the chasms between individuals and communities. This cycle breeds animosity, leading to conflict, and hindering progress towards a more harmonious world.

Judgment is a heavy burden to bear. It colors our perception, tainting our interactions and relationships. As we judge others, we also subject ourselves to harsh self-criticism. The relentless pursuit of perceived perfection creates an environment of constant discontentment and self-loathing. This weight stifles creativity, impedes personal growth, and fosters a sense of unworthiness.

Amidst the gloomy clouds of judgment, a glimmer of hope awaits. Releasing judgment offers the possibility of profound transformation, not only for the individual but for the entire world. To release judgment is to unshackle ourselves from the chains of prejudice, bias, and ego-driven thinking.

At the core of releasing judgment lies the practice of empathy and compassion. When we suspend judgment and open our hearts to the experiences of others, we begin to see the common threads that connect us all. Empathy becomes a bridge that spans the divides, creating a fertile ground for understanding and healing.

As judgment recedes, unity flourishes. With unity comes the realization that we are all interconnected, bound by the delicate fabric of humanity. This sense of interconnectedness fuels collaboration and cooperation, as we recognize that our collective success is intertwined.

Releasing judgment allows us to embrace the beauty of diversity and champion inclusivity.

When we celebrate our differences rather than fear them, we enrich our lives and create a vibrant tapestry of cultures, perspectives, and ideas.

Individuals who embody non-judgmental attitudes become beacons of light in a world shrouded in darkness. They serve as catalysts for change, inspiring others to follow suit. Leading by example, they plant seeds of transformation in hearts and minds, igniting a collective movement towards a more compassionate and accepting society.

The release of judgment is not an isolated act; it is a global movement that carries the potential to reshape our world. When societies collectively prioritize empathy, understanding, and compassion, systems begin to shift. Institutions, policies, and cultures evolve to reflect a newfound commitment to equity and justice.

Releasing judgment empowers individuals to make more conscious choices. Freed from the burden of prejudice, people can approach decisions with clarity and integrity. Such empowered choices ripple through every aspect of life, creating a harmonious and benevolent ripple effect.

Central to releasing judgment is the acceptance of imperfection, both in ourselves and others. Rather than striving for unattainable ideals, we embrace our humanity and recognize that growth and learning often arise from the embrace of imperfection.

The transformative power of releasing judgment is a profound force that has the potential to reshape the world as we know it. By suspending judgment, cultivating empathy, and embracing diversity, individuals can contribute to a ripple effect of positive change that spans continents and generations. As we release judgment, we embrace a world of unity, collaboration, and collective growth, unlocking the boundless potential of humanity's interconnected spirit.

Releasing judgment not only transforms the world on a macroscopic scale but also facilitates personal healing. For both the one who judges and the one who is judged, judgment is a source of pain and disconnection. However, when we let go of our preconceptions, we open the door to healing wounded relationships and fostering reconciliation. It allows us to see beyond the surface and delve into the true essence of the other person, acknowledging their struggles and triumphs without harsh labels.

Communication, the lifeblood of human interaction, undergoes a remarkable evolution when judgment dissipates. Listening becomes an act of genuine curiosity and understanding rather than a tool for formulating responses or reinforcing our own beliefs. In the absence of judgment, conversations become more open, honest, and compassionate, nurturing deeper connections between individuals.

Releasing judgment empowers individuals to embrace their own personal growth journeys. When we stop comparing ourselves to others and critiquing our every move, we liberate ourselves from the constraints of societal expectations. This newfound freedom allows us to explore our true passions, strengths, and weaknesses, fostering a profound sense of self-discovery and growth.

In a world where judgment is released, conflict resolution takes on a transformative hue. Instead of seeking to impose blame or perpetuate animosity, the focus shifts towards understanding the root causes of conflicts. Empathy and compassion become integral tools in addressing grievances, paving the way for peaceful resolutions and reconciliation.

The impact of releasing judgment extends beyond the current generation. As we cultivate empathy and compassion in ourselves and the next generation, we lay the foundation for a new breed of empathetic leaders who prioritize the well-being of their communities and the world at large. These leaders value cooperation over competition and seek to bridge gaps rather than widen divides.

A culture that embraces non-judgment nurtures an environment of acceptance, where individuals feel safe to express their authentic selves. It encourages creativity, innovation, and divergent thinking, as people are less afraid of criticism and more willing to take risks.

When a critical mass of individuals releases judgment, the power of collective consciousness ignites a global shift. As more people awaken to the transformative potential of non-judgment, the energy of compassion and empathy amplifies, spilling over into every aspect of society.

In the light of non-judgment, the world is reborn. Borders become blurred as people recognize their shared humanity and interconnectedness. The artificial divisions that once fueled conflicts are replaced by a celebration of diversity and an embrace of unity.

In this transformed world, compassion becomes the currency of interactions, and empathy bridges gaps between cultures, nations, and generations. Conflict gives way to collaboration, and inclusivity paves the path towards progress and innovation. As judgment dissipates, love and understanding flourish, leaving a lasting legacy for generations to come.

The act of releasing judgment is not a passive endeavor but a courageous and transformative journey that can revolutionize the world. It calls upon each of us to look within ourselves, confront our biases, and choose empathy over prejudice. By releasing judgment, we unlock the boundless potential of humanity, creating a world of harmony, unity, and profound interconnectedness. Let us embark on this transformative path, confident in the knowledge that every step we take towards non-judgment is a step closer to a brighter, more compassionate future for all.

Conclusion

In the depths of human existence lies an innate desire to connect with others, to understand, and to be understood. Yet, as we traverse the intricate pathways of life, our encounters with various beliefs, opinions, and behaviors can sometimes lead us astray. One of the most common pitfalls we encounter on this journey is the insidious tendency to judge others based on our limited perspectives and preconceived notions.

Amidst this tumultuous backdrop, the notion of operating in the love of God emerges as a beacon of hope, guiding us toward a more profound and transformative way of relating to the world around us. When we embrace the love of God, we recognize the interconnectedness of all living beings and the divine essence that resides within each soul. In doing so, we liberate ourselves from the shackles of judgment, embracing compassion, understanding, and empathy instead.

Judgment is a product of our inner landscape – the culmination of our beliefs, values, and past experiences. Often arising from feelings of superiority or fear, it masks itself as a tool for discernment, protecting us from perceived threats or upholding our standards of righteousness. However, in its wake, judgment isolates, divides, and perpetuates a cycle of negativity, affecting not only those we assess but also our own emotional well-being.

Operating in the love of God calls for a radical shift in perspective – one that acknowledges the inherent worth of every being. In every heart, there exists a divine spark, a connection to the Creator that transcends all differences. By seeing this divinity in others, we move beyond judgment and seek common ground, fostering unity and understanding.

When we operate in the love of God, we embrace empathy and compassion as guiding principles. Empathy allows us to stand in another's shoes, experiencing their joys, struggles, and fears firsthand. Compassion arises from this empathic connection, compelling us to extend kindness and support without the need for judgment.

To operate in the love of God does not imply that we abandon discernment altogether. Instead, we learn to discern without condemning. We recognize that every individual is on their unique journey, influenced by a myriad of factors beyond our understanding. Our task is not to label them as good or bad, right or wrong, but rather to offer a helping hand, a listening ear, or a gentle nudge in the direction of growth and transformation.

At the heart of judgment lies the ego – that part of us that seeks validation, superiority, and control. To break free from judgment's clutches, we must embark on an inner journey of self-awareness and introspection. Through self-awareness, we recognize the ego's influence on our thoughts and actions, enabling us to respond from a place of love rather than egoic reactivity.

In the realm of love, forgiveness reigns supreme. When we truly embrace the love of God, forgiveness becomes a natural response to perceived wrongs. We understand that harboring resentment and judgment only shackles us to the past, preventing us from experiencing the fullness of the present moment.

Operating in the love of God does not demand uniformity but celebrates diversity. We learn to appreciate the various facets of humanity, recognizing that each unique perspective enriches the tapestry of existence. Our differences no longer serve as walls that divide but as bridges that connect us in profound and meaningful ways.

When we operate in the love of God, we undergo a profound transformation that liberates us from the burden of judgment. We become ambassadors of love, spreading empathy, compassion, and understanding wherever we go. Embracing the divine spark within each being, we cultivate unity amidst diversity and embark on a journey of self-discovery and inner peace. May this divine love guide our steps as we navigate the intricate dance of life, illuminating the path toward a world free from judgment and overflowing with love.

In our pursuit of love and understanding, mindfulness becomes a powerful ally. By practicing mindfulness, we train our minds to be fully present, to observe our thoughts and emotions without immediate judgment. Through this practice, we cultivate a heightened awareness of our biases and preconceptions, enabling us to respond with love and acceptance rather than react with judgment.

Gratitude acts as a bridge between ourselves and others, leading us closer to the love of God. When we appreciate the blessings and gifts life has bestowed upon us, we foster a heart filled with abundance. In this state of gratitude, our inclination to judge diminishes, and we begin to see the beauty in the uniqueness of each individual.

Operating in the love of God calls us to embrace a love that transcends conditions and expectations. Unconditional love does not hinge on someone's behavior, beliefs, or actions; rather, it emanates from a place of unwavering acceptance and compassion. In practicing unconditional love, we free ourselves from the chains of judgment, for we understand that everyone, including ourselves, is deserving of love and forgiveness.

To extend love and compassion to others authentically, we must first cultivate self-compassion. Often, we are our harshest critics, quick to judge ourselves for our perceived flaws and mistakes. When we learn to be kind and gentle with ourselves, embracing our imperfections with understanding, we become better equipped to extend the same grace to others.

Judgment often arises from our desire to control outcomes and people. However, as we surrender the illusion of control, we open ourselves to a more profound experience of love and acceptance. We understand that every individual has their unique path, and it is not for us to dictate or enforce upon them.

Operating in the love of God requires a willingness to be vulnerable, both with ourselves and with others. Vulnerability allows us to break down barriers, inviting genuine connections and fostering an environment of trust and mutual understanding. When we embrace vulnerability, we recognize that it is a strength, not a weakness, and it empowers us to see the vulnerability in others with empathy and tenderness.

In a world often marked by divisiveness and polarization, the love of God becomes a powerful force to transcend tribalism and bridge the gaps that separate us. It reminds us that beneath our external identities and affiliations, we are all interconnected beings, sharing the same human experience. By operating in love, we seek unity, embracing the diversity that enriches our shared journey.

To truly embody the love of God, we must collectively work towards creating a culture of love and acceptance. This involves fostering environments that encourage open dialogue, active listening, and the recognition of our shared humanity. It calls for conscious efforts to eradicate prejudice, bias, and discrimination, both within ourselves and society at large.

In conclusion, operating in the love of God is not a passive endeavor but an active and transformative way of being in the world. It requires us to continuously cultivate self-awareness, compassion, and understanding. As we liberate ourselves from the confines of judgment, we find freedom and peace within ourselves and sow seeds of love that have the power to transform the world around us. Let us embrace the love of God with open hearts, for in doing so, we unleash a force of unity and compassion that knows no bounds.

ABOUT THE AUTHOR

Dr. Jeremy Lopez is Founder and President of Identity Network and Now Is Your Moment. Identity Network is one of the world's leading prophetic resource sites, offering books, teachings, and courses to a global audience. For more than thirty years, Dr. Lopez has been considered a pioneering voice within the field of the prophetic arts and his proven strategies for success coaching are now being implemented by various training groups and faith groups throughout the world. Dr. Lopez is the author of more than forty books, including his international bestselling books The Universe is at Your Command and Creating with Your Thoughts. Throughout his career, he has spoken prophetically into the lives of heads of business as well as heads of state. He has ministered to Governor Bob Riley of the State of Alabama, Prime Minister Benjamin Netanyahu, and Shimon Peres. Dr. Lopez continues to be a highly sought conference teacher and host, speaking on the topics of human potential and spirituality.

ADDITIONAL WORKS

The Processes of God

SEERS: The Eyes of the Kingdom

The Universe is at your Command: Vibrating the Creative Side of God

How Does God Speak?

And many more...

PROPHETIC READINGS

What is the Holy Spirit saying about your future? Find out by scheduling your personal prophecy with Dr. Jeremy Lopez today. To schedule your prophetic reading, contact the office of Identity Network at www.identitynetwork.net.

Made in the USA
Columbia, SC
02 September 2023